I0086214

MASTERS OF INTROSPECTION AN INTEGRATIVE THESIS ON SUFFERING

DOUG McPHILLIPS

Also, by Doug McPhillips:

NOVELS. AND ALBUMS

From Darkness to Light
Awake to My Gutted Dreams
he Sword of Discernment
Santiago Traveller
I Prophet: towards 2030
Masters at my table
The Guru of Jerusalem
We is me Upside Down (Biography)
The Wicklow Way
The Adventures of Ace McDice,
 Stretch Deed & Moonshine Melody
Instant Karma & Grace
The Credo
Reflections of an Old Man
A Writer on the Rocks
Reincarnation of the Assassin
Master of the Arts
The Songs, not the Singer
To Whom it May Concern
A Camino Guide Book
Country Camino (Album)
Santiago Traveller (Album)
Soul Fact.(Album

Doug McPhillips April 2024 ISBN. 978-0-6486214-64

Content.

Introduction. Page 5.

Chapter 1. Edifying Suffering Self. Page 7.

Chapter 2. Old Testament trials & tribulations. Page 15.

Chapter 3. Trials of King David. Page 23.

Chapter 4. Jesus Miracles and Suffering. Page 31.

Chapter 5 Peter the Rock. Page 43.

Chapter 6. Paul, the Evangelist. Page 51.

Chapter 7. Being patient in Suffering. Page 59.

Chapter 8. Suffering as Christ's followers.Page 67.

Chapter 9. Refining Gold & Pruning Vines. Page 75.

Chapter 10. The Shadow Self in our Nature. Page 85.

Chapter 11. To Cry in the Suffering Christ. Page 99.

Chapter 12. Epilogue. Page 111.

Introspection is the examination of one's conscious thoughts and feelings. In psychology, the process of introspection relies on observing one's mental state, while in a spiritual context, it may refer to examining one's soul.

Introduction.

Henry David Thoreau, naturalist, American poet and philosopher, once stated in his writings: "The mass of men lead lives of quiet desperation. What is called resignation is confirmed desperation. From the desperate city you go into the desperate country and have to console yourself with the bravery of minks and muskrats. A stereotype of unconscious despair is concealed even under what we call the games and amusements of man. There is no play in them, for this comes after work. But it is a characteristic of wisdom not to do desperate things."

In another quote, Thoreau stated: "If a man does not keep pace with his companions, perhaps it is because he hears a different drummer. Let him step to the music he hears however measured or far away."

There comes a time for every man to search deep within, beyond the desperation and despair, pain, suffering and heartache, beyond the passing sense of feelings of joy and temporary elation of worldly relief, to search the heart, the soul of self for the answers to our purpose, to a sense of knowing what one's individual and collective game plan is. This little work examines the viewpoint of historical figures from a religious, philosophical, and academic point of view to find a template to use in one's conclusions.

The writer uses this opportunity to state his case, having drawn upon historical figures, his own life experience, and those to whom he had turned, to set a course best suited to living life for an inner purpose. This author has been awakened to a life's calling that he was unaware of for most of his former days. It was through the slings and arrows of outrageous fortune during his lifetime that he came to these conclusions. Like most humans, he only realised his true purpose late in life.

It is hoped in the body of this work that you, the reader, will find some benefit as a guiding light to awaken your souls purpose if you have yet to see it. If nothing else, it may well soothe the savage beast that lay within, help to elevate your suffering and enlighten the benefits of understanding the answers that have come from many historical figures drawn upon in the stories within.

CHAPTER 1.

EDIFYING SUFFERING SELF

Each individual, at some time or another, experiences suffering, either physically or mentally. Later chapters will examine historical figures who experienced great suffering and found faith and enlightenment. Meanwhile, this chapter examines the effects of the suffering of an individual, namely me, to provide some sense and sensibility into the reasons for my suffering and the outcomes of a positive and enlightening nature resulting from the night of my soul.

How a person looks at, encounters, and overcomes psychological, mental, social, and even spiritual suffering makes all the difference. No achiever succeeds without passing through a phase of struggle in life. A battle may be short-lived or extended in days or even years. Sufferings do not always mean bloodshed, violence or physical suffering, but they can take the forms of agony, angst, psychological trauma, depression and turbulence. Suffering is an inescapable predicament in human life. For some, it came after much heartache and pain; for others, it was always there despite not understanding why they were to suffer.

An observer may understand a person's transformation from suffering regarding the cultivation and exercise of the virtues of being *edified*

Ian James Kidd of the Department of Philosophy of Durham University, UK, wrote a paper entitled Transformative Suffering and the Cultivation of Virtue. Here are some of his conclusions, which I have modified for ease of expression.

"The idea that specific experiences of suffering can be positively transformative has a central role in the edification of the spirit self of Christian theology. It is easy to identify different historical and doctrinal reasons why physical, mental, and spiritual suffering is central to that traditional belief but less accessible in practical and pastoral aspects of Christian theology. i.e., to articulate and justify the provocative claim that suffering can be positively transformative. Indeed, some critics protest that the *very idea* is deeply offensive on moral, theological, and psychological grounds, and those critics have included many Christian laypeople and theologians.

Christian ethics has a robust virtue-ethical tradition that recognises virtues, such as humility and tolerance, that educationists often appeal to in each case because those virtues are responses to the inherent frailty of the human condition. In his writings, St Augustine urged Christians to make 'wise and appropriate use' of their illnesses to 'exercise humility' by appreciating the 'frailty of mortal flesh'. Historically, scholars testify their experiences of suffering led to the cultivation of virtues - of 'greater trust' and 'stronger hope' – and to the ways that they had undergone 'purification' of their souls'. Edification similarly involves purging vices and perfecting virtue as part of a richer process of moral self-cultivation that is apt to be described using a spiritual vocabulary of self-purification. Indeed, this vision informs the venerable conception of philosophy as a 'way of life' or set of 'spiritual practices' that scholars have attributed to the Hellenistic philosophies that informed the early development of Christian theology. The core claim of an edification conception of suffering is that specific experiences can afford distinctive opportunities for cultivating and exercising *virtues*."

"My account of an edifying conception of illness draws upon the phenomenological model of illness developed by Havi Carel. In that model, the affliction of the suffering soul may reach a state that involves the diminishing and disappearance of cognitive, physical, and social capacity and the gradual loss of the sufferer's mobility, memory, social capacity, etc.

Carel argues two forms of response to capacity loss in illness: the first consists of familiar biomedical reactions, such as surgery or drug regimens, and the second consists of 'positive responses', including 'adaptability' and 'creativity'. Such positive responses involve the ill person adjusting their attitudes and activities to ameliorate or minimise the negative impact of capacity loss upon their life, such as adapting their daily routine or creatively identifying new ways to perform old tasks. Carel concludes that such positive responses to the malady of suffering can allow an ill person to achieve a 'modified but rich texture of life'. I suggest that Carel's claims reflect a latent intellectual instruction   since positive responses to illness are interpretable as cultivating and exercising virtues in a positively morally transformative or edifying way."

There are three claims in common to moral teaching and post-traumatic theologies. First, each emphasises the intrinsically harmful character of suffering despite its positive edifying potential. Second, each highlights that suffering is only potentially edifying or transformative, such that one's suffering is not an inevitable source of positive transformation. Third, both moral teaching and post-traumatic theologies accentuate that the positive potential of suffering is contingent upon the sufferers' *response* to their suffering. My account of edification is the core claim that certain persons can respond to their experiences of illness in positively transformative ways.

The first is that *transformation* can be understood in terms of the cultivation and exercise of virtues—of being edified—in a way supported by Christian theology and the case studies of post-traumatic theories. The second is that sufferers testify to how their experiences of suffering led to the cultivation of virtues - of 'greater trust' and 'stronger hope' – and to the ways that they had undergone 'purification' and of 'filling [of] their souls'.

My claim is that reflective experiences of any kind of suffering can fundamentally transform a person's understanding of and engagement with the world and, indeed, with God.

A Christian who experiences transformative suffering recognises that it offers positive potential and responds by cultivating and exercising various ethical and spiritual virtues – either as a personal, private process or under the guidance of a pastoral leader. This edifying process is triply transformative: first, being edified involves a transformation of how one can cope with suffering through what Carel calls a *positive response*; second, being edified means being morally and spiritually transformed through the purgation of vice and the perfection of virtue; third, being edified ultimately involves a transformation of how a person experiences and engages with the world, including the adoption of newly virtuous sensibilities and dispositions that radically transform one's way of being in the world—hence the 'insight, compassion and beauty."

"—thus explaining the multimodal character of transformative suffering. A Christian, then, may find edification brings with it a triple sense of dependence: first, on one's moral peers and pastoral leaders who contributed to one's edification; second, on the moral and spiritual heritage that provides the resources that make edification possible; and third, on God as the source of goodness and ultimate source of moral purpose and authority. This triple sense of dependence - moral, spiritual, and metaphysical nature of being - is also arguably consonant with the central Christian virtue of *humility*. The suffering person, humbled by their experiences, can undergo a moral and spiritual transformation in which they cultivate virtues that grant new sensibilities and dispositions - ethical and spiritual, existential and aesthetic – that subsequently ultimately reveal to them the truth of their radical dependence upon the moral order and spiritual tradition established by God."

In light of what you have just read, it is hoped that in telling my story, what happened, what changed, and what it is like now, you will have some semblance of enlightened understanding of your particular life purpose and appreciate the edification of the soul, the creative spirit's influence over the presence of egocentric living in this world but not of it. Of working one's God-given talents for the benefit of the masses of mankind in preference to self-gratification of the ego, monetary rewards, and superstar hero status, which I had worked so hard to attain in a prior life.

In saying this, let it be understood that I have been a broken man as a result of the tragic circumstances of a past life that in no small way changed me, my beliefs and how I now cope with living the life that I now live. I am not cured but chastened as a consequence and continue to be in a state of recovery. In telling my story of progress but not perfection, I seek to write it now as a final epilogue, for I do not wish to continue repeatedly playing the same tapes. It is time to move on, to let it all go. Still, in the hope that you gain benefit from it, I shall tell it just one more time, for it is a fitting way to end this chapter and introduce the stories of suffering souls who, throughout history, have suffered much and through life lessons and introspective searching have found their way to a better life as consequence.

Whilst I had given up smoking cigarettes in my early married days, the constant episodes of drinking continued. I, like my drinking escapades in my misspent youth, had convinced myself that I had control over my alcohol consumption. Interestingly, I had planted my ladder up against the material world firmly, and in my mistaken belief, climbed more than once over a lifetime to the top only to find that when I got there it was empty, and I was alone. It did not seem to matter if it was the corporate ladder I climbed in the past or the ones I climbed working for myself; the result was the same. Something had to change to break the marble of my heart that was so firmly fixed on a hedonistic pathway to rack and ruin. It came in many unexpected ways, all in one year. The marriage had been breaking down over several years, but in my blindness I thought that proving material possessions would solve the unhappy state of affairs in time.

Then, one day, the mother of my children left me for another, and all of my life for the next decade turned pear-shaped. Over the ensuing twelve months, ten tragic events quickly followed. Not the least of these was the suicide of my second eldest son. Fair-wealthier friends left me; others died unexpectedly, and all the material wealth that I had striven so hard for turned to ashes. I tried to mend my broken self by turning to booze, which acted as a bandaid for a time but ultimately sent me spiralling into depression and rehabilitation. Fortunately, I stopped drinking recovered from depression with the help of antidepressants for a time and, ultimately, Alcoholics Anonymous. I have since managed to stay sober through the Steps of the programme and the spiritual concepts taught by AA, which I have since learnt to live by. During my recovery, I walked the Camino Way and, out of my brokenness, found my way back to a way of life I had never thought possible.

I had ventured for the first time on the Camino Way without a plan or goal. I had lots more to suffer and would walk The Way three times and attend two more rehabilitations over the next decade before the logical, linear half-brain notions would give way to a God of my understanding in a mystical and magical way of belief in an Infinite Intelligence that had made all. It was as if this Humpty Dumpty man climbed back upon a new wall of understanding. In time this manifested belief of the creative imagination came to the reality that both the logical, linear brain and the creative brain are a united body and that all my AA fellows are as one with me in their concepts of living in this world but not of it, at least in a spiritual sense.

Whilst I was on the Camino de Santiago pilgrimage for the first time, the power of the creative imagination took hold in a not-so-conventional way for me. It came first through a fall in Paris, resulting in cracking my head on the entrance floor of the hotel in which I was staying. The next day I was on a train to the Pyrenees mountains to begin my pilgrimage. Once settled on board the train, I started journaling my experience as a daily habit, which continued throughout the next month of my tramping the way of St. James on the Camino de Santiago.

My head throbbed from the knock I had taken the previous evening at the hotel, so I began to write a poem to distract my attention from my headache. Often, cathartic events result from suffering, which is critical to one's future. This was the case for me as I wrote about the life of my favourite grandfather, his time rounding up rangy cattle on horseback in the New England Ranges, and the stories he had told me as a small boy of his many adventures through a colourful lifetime. Once I completed the poem, I tucked the diary away in my backpack and thought no more about it until fate guided me along the pathway of my future life. Whilst I had fallen down the pit of darkness and despair in my former life, afraid to enter the dragon's mouth that seemed to be at the base of my inner self,

I soon found that God takes his stance in the matter if one has the patience to trust in his slow work.

It was some 400 kilometres into my Camino that the catalyst for a new way of life would be laid upon me. I had been walking with a German rock musician who, one evening played a ballad he had written relating to a refugee's fate. After he had finished singing, I casually mentioned that I had written a poem, a ballad of sorts on the first day of my Camino. He asked me to recite it to him, and he listened with interest to the story of my grandfather. He said very little at the time, but a month after my return home to Australia, he emailed me asking for the lyrics as he planned to write music to it and record it on his next album. I replied that I had no chorus for it yet and promised to send it to him when I came up with one. Meanwhile, I sent him two other poems instead. The musician Robin Marien from Master Mint's group recorded and wrote the chords of one of those poems and ultimately the song about my grandfather soon followed.

I realised then then I could write songs. So, arising from that pit of hell that I emerged from the dragon's mouth, and a lotus flower of creative ideas followed. Over the next decade, I walked the Camino de Santiago three times, tramping over hills and valleys in Ireland, New Zealand, and Australia. What has emerged are three albums of my songs to date and twenty books of various genres that sell both locally and worldwide. I have no claim to fame due to my creative efforts, instead write books and songs for the benefit of you, and and this 'wordsmith.' It is a gift granted by God for me and you, where fate has taken a hand to turn my former life into something beneficial for the well-being of my soul and yours. So it is as a consequence of the dark night of the soul that I emerged in the dawning light to a rebirth of awakening and equal vulnerability in a response through creative outpouring in solidarity with others who suffer and who can take some solace from the gift I have been granted.

CHAPTER 2.

OLD TESTAMENT TRIALS & TRIBULATIONS

The story of Job, a man whose friends show up after he suffers significant losses to justify the apparent actions of God on him, is the story of a man whose stance before God is not one so much of patience in the face of unexplainable and unjustfied suffering, but of defiant stance. God's presence at the end says as much: Job was correct; he did not deserve the suffering he underwent. God witnesses our world's unjust violence and suffering by showing up and addressing Job. Pain can be transformed, from this viewpoint and transformed from being wholly meaningless into something constitutive of a new humanity. This is despite its completely unjustifiable nature, as with Job's suffering.

Job's insurrection against God—his 'nature of being resistance', as some have put it—'admits the failure and inadequacy of old standards of justice,' offering us the failure of God's violence and perceived strength at the same time as it promises new solidarities among those who suffer for no apparent reason. This reconfiguration of the oldest theological themes on suffering is Job's testament to humanity. It ultimately lays the foundations for Jesus's later reconfiguration of the law—the very transfiguration Peter had first missed, as you will find in a chapter that follows.

The Book of Job is a text within both the Christian and Jewish canons that tells the story of Job, a wealthy man chosen for a test by God. Satan claims that Job is only a faithful man because God has blessed him with wealth and a large family, so God agrees to let Satan take everything from Job.

Job, a righteous, God-fearing man, experiences severe trials and afflictions due to God's will and the devil's influence. He loses his property, his children die, and he suffers great physical agony. Amid his suffering, Job is visited by three friends. Though Job's friends intend to comfort him, they accuse him of transgression.

Regrettably, Job's friends cannot endure the mystery of his suffering, so they jump to conclusions about its source. The first of the three, Eliphaz,,a character from the book of Genesis, acknowledges that Job has been a source of strength to others (Job 4:3-4). But then he turns and blames Job's suffering squarely on Job himself. "Think now," he says, "who that innocent ever perished? Or where were the upright cut off? As I have seen, those who plough iniquity and sow trouble reap the same"(Job 4: 7-8). Job's second friend, Bildad, says much the same. "See, God will not reject a blameless person nor take the hand of evildoers" (Job 8: 20) The third friend, Zophar, repeats the refrain. "If iniquity is in your hand, put it far away; do not let wickedness reside in your tents. Surely, you will lift your face without blemish and be secure and not afraid.... Your life will be brighter than the noonday" (Job: 11:14-17, 17).

Their reasoning is a syllogism. God sends calamities upon wicked people only. You have suffered a calamity. Therefore, you must be wicked. Job himself avoids this false syllogism. But it is very commonly accepted by Christians. It is called a theology of divine retribution, assuming God blesses those faithful to him and punishes those who sin. It is only partially with biblical support. There are many cases in which God sends calamity as a punishment, as he did at Sodom (Genesis 19:1-29). Often, our experiences do bear out this theological position. In most situations, things turn out better when we follow God's ways than when we forsake them. However, God does not *always* work that way. Jesus himself pointed out that disaster is not necessarily a sign of God's judgment (Luke 13:4). In Job's case, we know the theology of divine retribution is not true because God says that Job is a righteous man (Job 1:8. 2.3). Job's friends' devastating error is to apply a generalisation to Job's situation, without knowing what they're talking about. Anyone who has spent time with a suffering friend knows how hard it is to remain present without trying to give answers. It is excruciating to suffer silently with a friend who must rebuild life piece by piece without any certainty about the outcome. Our instinct is to investigate what went wrong and identify a solution. Then, we can help our friend eliminate the cause and return to normal as soon as possible. Knowing the cause, we will at least know how to avoid the same fate ourselves. We would instead give a reason for the suffering — be it right or wrong —than accept the mystery at the heart of suffering.

Job's friends succumb to this temptation. It would be foolish to imagine that we would never do the same. How much harm have well-intentioned Christians caused by giving pious-sounding answers to suffering, even though we have no idea what we're talking about? "It's all for the best." "It's part of God's plan." "God never sends people more adversity than they can handle." How arrogant to imagine we know God's plan. How foolish to think we know the reason for anyone else's suffering. We don't even know the reason for our suffering. It would be more truthful and helpful to admit, "I don't know why this happened to you. No one should have to go through this." If we can do this and *remain present*, we may become an agent of God's compassion.

Job's friends can't lament with Job or even acknowledge that they lack a basis for judging him. They are hell-bent (literally, given Satan's role) on defending God by placing the blame on Job. As the friends' speeches continue, their rhetoric becomes increasingly hostile. Faced with the self-imposed choice of blaming Job or God, they harden their hearts against their former friend. "There is no end to your iniquities," says Eliphaz, one of Job's comforters (Job 22:5), and then he invents some iniquities to charge against Job. "You have given no water to the weary to drink, and you have withheld bread from the hungry" (Job 22:7). "You have sent widows away empty-handed, and the arms of the orphans you have crushed" (Job 22:9)

Zophar's last speech observes that wicked persons will not enjoy their riches because God will make their stomachs "vomit them up again"(Job 20:15) and that "They will give back the fruit of their toil, and will not swallow it down; from the profit from their trading they will get no fruit of their enjoyment" (Job 20: 18). This is an appropriate righting of the wicked's wrongdoing, that "they have crushed and abandoned the poor, they have seized a house that they did not build"(Job 20:19). . The reader knows this does not apply to Job. Why is Zophar so eager to blame Job? Are we sometimes too eager to follow in Zophar's footsteps when our friends face failures in work and life?

The book of Job demands that we see ourselves in the faces of Job's friends. We, too — presumably — know right from wrong and have some sense of God's ways. But we do not know God's ways as they apply in all times and places. "Such knowledge is too wonderful for me; it is so high that I cannot attain it" (Psalm 139:6). God's ways are often a mystery beyond our understanding. Is it possible that we also are guilty of ignorant judgments against our friends and co-workers?

But it doesn't have to be friends who accuse us. Unlike Job, most of us are quite ready to accuse ourselves. Anyone who has tasted failure has likely pondered, "What have I done to deserve this?" It's natural and not altogether incorrect. Sometimes, out of sheer laziness, bad data or incompetence, we make poor decisions that cause us to fail at work. However, not all failures are the direct result of our shortcomings. Many are the result of circumstances outside our control. Workplaces are complex, with many factors competing for our attention, many ambiguous situations, and many decisions where the outcomes are impossible to predict. How do we know whether we are always following God's ways? How could we or anyone genuinely know whether our successes and failures are due to our actions or to factors beyond our control? How could an outsider judge the rightness of our actions without knowing the intimate details of our situations? Indeed, how could we even judge ourselves, given the limits of our knowledge?

Job claimed that God had fallen asleep at the wheel of the universe, and because of this divine neglect, he had to endure unjust suffering. However, it clearly states that Job never lost faith in God and forever called to God in prayer, asking Him to remove his affliction: And [mention] Job, when he called to his Lord, "Indeed, adversity has touched me, and you are the Most Merciful of the merciful."

Ultimately, God restored all that Job had lost and gave Him twice as much as before. The Lord blessed him with a long life and seven more sons and three more daughters who were the most beautiful women in all the land!

Maybe Job's moral is this: If God doesn't create just circumstances, then we have to, as we do. In the face of a harsh, collapsing world and the ignorant devotion that worsens it, Job's honesty must be our guiding force. Seven lessons from the Book of Job are worthy of mention here. Firstly, God vindicates Himself in the end; second, God is the proven sovereign over all suffering; third, we express our faith through sorrow and weeping. fourth, Don't be like Job's friends; fifth, learn from what they did right; sixth, be patient with the sufferer; and seventh, accurately apply Scripture to your enlightenment.

Even more puzzling in introspection is the meaning of life itself, for better or worse, in the scheme of things. No better example in the Old Testament Bible is the Ecclesiastics narration.

The words of the Teacher, son of David, king in Jerusalem:

"Meaningless! Meaningless!"
 says the Teacher.
"Utterly meaningless!
 Everything is meaningless."

What do people gain from all their labor?
 at which they toil under the sun?
Generations come, and generations go,
but the earth remains forever.

the sun rises, and the sun sets,·
 and hurries back to where it rises.
The wind blows to the south
 and turns to the north;
round and round it goes,
 ever returning on its course.
All streams flow into the sea,
 yet the sea is never full.
To the place the streams come from,
 there they return.

Is there anything of which one can say,
 "Look! This is something new"?
It was here already, long ago;
 It was here before our time

No one remembers the former generations,
 and even those yet to come
will not be remembered
 by those who follow them."

The King was speaking on introspection of the meaning of his life. "I, the Teacher, was king over Israel in Jerusalem. I applied my mind to study and explore all that is done under the heavens by wisdom. What a heavy burden God has laid on mankind! I have seen everything done under the sun; all are meaningless, chasing after the wind. What is crooked cannot be straightened; what is lacking cannot be counted."

I said, "Look, I have increased in wisdom more than anyone who has ruled over Jerusalem before me; I have experienced much wisdom and knowledge." Then I applied myself to the understanding of wisdom, madness, and folly, but I learned that this, too, is chasing after the wind.

What do workers gain from their toil? I have seen the burden God has laid on the human race. He has made everything beautiful in its time. He has also set eternity in the human heart, yet no one can fathom what God has done from beginning to end. I know that there is nothing better for people than to be happy and to do good while they live. Each of them may eat and drink and find satisfaction in all their toil—this is the gift of God.I know that everything God does will endure forever; nothing can be added to it, and nothing can be taken from it. God does it so that people will fear him."

I also said to myself, "As for humans, God tests them so that they may see that they are like animals. Surely, the fate of human beings is like that of the animals; the same fate awaits them both: As one dies, so dies the other. All have the same breath; humans have no advantage over animals. Everything is meaningless."

The book of Ecclesiastes is unique because although the Teacher is a believer, he often poses questions and makes statements as if he were not. Everything that he says, therefore, must be taken in the context of his conclusion in Ecclesiastes 12:13-14 that all of our works in this life will one day be judged by God. The teachings of this book seem to be directed at individuals who do not believe in God or at least are not yet fully committed to Him.

The teacher presents questions and statements that many of these individuals may feel inclined to agree with, but then he helps them see how much purpose and meaning can come into our lives when we seek to live by God's will.

CHAPTER 3.

TRIALS OF KING DAVID

The Teacher in the story of Job presents questions and statements that many of these individuals may feel inclined to agree with, but then he helps them see how much purpose and meaning can come into our lives when we seek to live by God's will. Such a theme is presented in the trails of King David too.

King David was forever troubled by suffering and difficulties. He was hounded and harassed all through his life, at first by the King, who was the most powerful of all men in his country, and later, even by his own progeny. So David had to hide in a cave, in the mountains, and on the outskirts of the desert and flee from city to city. Though he moved from place to place, his only shelter was God.

In Psalm 55, he compares himself to a dove that flies away and finds solace, "Oh, that I had the wings of a dove! I would fly away and be at rest". We know of the suffering he undergoes at various times - King Saul sent him to fight a heavily armed Philistine giant, who reportedly would kill every armed man of King Saul's army had they been willing to face him. After 40 days Saul ultimately sent David, who volunteered to face the giant Goliath armed only with a slingshot and stone. David, with skilful aim and with the belief that with God, nothing is impossible, hit the giant in the temple with a stone and killed him instantly.

David was suffering many afflictions at the time. He turned to God in prayer for comfort and awareness of God's love for him, which gave him the courage to persevere through much trouble and heartache. Despite his defects of character, trouble and strife, he acknowledged the need to ' man up, ' as it were, to what God's purpose was for him.

In meditative prayer, David asked for God's forgiveness and mercy. He recognised God's love for him and asked to be cleansed from all his wrongdoing. In a sense, he had unmasked his egocentricity and was reaching a 'pure state' in following the word of his heavenly Father, despite his suffering and his shortcomings.

Search me, O God, and know my heart! Try me and know my thoughts!
And see if there be any grievous way in me,
and lead me in the way everlasting! – Psalm 139: 23-24

David lived in violent times and went to battle as a foot soldier for King Saul in his younger years and later as King himself, sending troops into battle. He saw his weakness and need for repentance irrespective of circumstance.

"Repentance requires honesty. No one comes to God with true repentance, first acknowledged their need for forgiveness and reconciliation with him. Only those who have ceased trying to cover up their sin with self-righteousness and deceit can experience the deep and lasting change that comes only through repentance."

"Have mercy on me, O God,
according to your unfailing love;
according to your great compassion
blot out my transgressions
Wash away all my iniquity and
cleanse me from my sin.

Deliver me from the guilt of bloodshed, O God,
you who are God my Saviour,
and my tongue will sing of your righteousness."
(Psalm 51:1,2,14).

King Saul, in one of his many episodes of being possessed by an evil spirit, was after David, who had fallen out of favour of the King at the time. So David was on the run. Doeg, King Saul and his family - is like a whirlwind, but those are the situations that birth his lyrics. Even God certifies him as "a man after his own heart."

In his escape, he stops for food at Nob, where the Ark resides in the ancient tabernacle. Ahimilech was a priest on duty. David asked for bread. In a historic move about which Jesus later would comment, Ahimilech gave him the loaves of the consecrated bread that sat that week on the table in the Holy Place. But David also needed a weapon. He had left with none at all. "Is there not a spear or a sword on hand?" Lying behind the ephod, a special priestly garment, was the spear of Goliath himself. "There is none like it; give it to me." And why wouldn't it be given to David, who killed Goliath a short time before?

Nestled in this fascinating text in 1 Samuel 22 are these foreboding words, "Now one of the servants of Saul was there that day, detained before the Lord; and his name was Doeg the Edomite, the chief of Saul's shepherds."

Thought Doeg was on King Saul's staff as chief shepherd, he was a traitor to his people. Israel and Edom were currently enemies (1 Sam 14:47). The statement, "detained by the Lord," does not improve our confidence in him either. It doesn't speak of Doeg's true devotion, for his heart was far from God, but speaks of his feigned religiosity among his adopted people.

Now move ahead to the tamarisk tree where King Saul sat with his own spear in his hand. He complained with his servants around him: "All of you have conspired against me… none of you is sorry for me." He openly griped about the covenant between David and Jonathan, his son, that had recently come to light, which fuelled even more jealousy and hatred toward David.

Then Doeg speaks up, a man ready with an inside word. "I saw the son of Jesse (David) coming to Nob, too Ahimelech He inquired of the Lord for him, gave him provisions, and gave him the sword of Goliath the Philistine."

That was all it took. Ahimilech, the priest, was summoned immediately by Saul, and he dutifully came with his entire household—many fellow priests. In a moment, he was tried and condemned to die, though he was an innocent man. But no servant of the King would do Saul's bidding, indicating that they were afraid to kill God's anointed priests or that they privately had sympathies for David.

But one man will do it: Doeg.

Doeg killed 85 priests that day, and "he struck Nob the city of the priests with the edge of the sword, both men and women, children and infants; also oxen, donkeys, and sheep he struck with the edge of the sword." Only a Doeg could be so thorough.

This episode ends when one priest, who had escaped, reports the slaughter to David. David's reply is sobering: " I knew on that day, when Doeg the Edomite was there, that he would surely tell Saul. I have brought about the death of every person in your father's household." David, "a man after God's own heart," was betrayed by Doeg, a man after Saul's own heart.

Moral: You cannot tell a man by where he worships, but only by his heart.

Later, when King Saul died and David ascended the throne, Absalom, his own flesh and blood, planed to kill David and take his throne. This makes David feel that his own sword has pierced his soul, and so he runs away to save his life:

Lord, how many are my foes!
How many rise up against me!
Many are saying of me,
"God will not deliver him."
But you, Lord, are a shield around me,
my glory, the One who lifts my head high.
I call the Lord, who answers me from his holy mountain. (3:1- 4)

David aspires to be with God, not only at the time of suffering, but he seeks God even after being delivered from his enemies.

The Lord is my rock, my fortress and my deliverer;
my God is my rock, in whom I take refuge,
my shield and the horn of my salvation, my stronghold.
I called to the Lord, who is worthy of praise,
and I have been saved from my enemies.
The cords of death entangled me;
The torrents of destruction overwhelmed me.
The cords of the grave coiled around me;
the snares of death confronted me. (18:2-5)

Despite all the pain and difficulty David faced he proved his worth in the eyes of God due to his great faith in his maker.

"The Spirit of the Lord spoke through me;
His words were on my tongue.

The God of Israel spoke,

the Rock of Israel said to me:
'When one rules over people in righteousness,
when he rules in the fear of God,

he is like the light of morning at sunrise
on a cloudless morning,
like the brightness after rain
that brings grass from the earth."
"If my house were not right with God,
 surely he would not have made with me an everlasting covenant,
 arranged and secured in every part;
 surely he would not bring to fruition my salvation

But evil men are all to be cast aside like thorns,
which are not gathered with the hand.

Whoever touches thorns
uses a tool of iron or the shaft of a spear;
they are burned up where they lie."

In the Old Testament, God made provision for cities of refuge so that a murder accused would have a second chance of hearing. He could run and hide himself there, and no one could lay his hand on him. Similarly, David finds shelter on so many occasions after sinning or when he flees from his enemies: he finds shelter in the wings of God, cries to God with a broken and contrite heart, seeks solace, gets convicted of his sins, receives pardon from God and regains his lost serenity and joy. Thus David sings Psalms that connect and find a better rapport with God." But take heart! I have overcome the world" (John 16:33).

There are many ways to reach peace, harmony, and relief, and one of the most effective is through the use of lyrics as David so used in his distress:

The Lord is my shepherd; I shall not want.
He makes me lie down in green pastures.
He leads me beside still waters.
He restores my soul.
He leads me in paths of righteousness
for his name's sake.

"The LORD is my shepherd; I shall not be in want. He restores my soul. He guides me in paths of righteousness for his name's sake. Even though I walk through the valley of the shadow of death, I will fear no evil, for you are with me; your rod and your staff, they comfort me."

It is important to notice that the words, "Thy rod and Thy staff comfort me" (Psalms 23:4, come immediately after the words, "Even though I walk through the valley of the shadow of death."

The psalmist plainly says that the shepherd's staff comforts him when he is under the fearful shadow of death. The threat of death, either to us personally or to a loved one, has caused many people to turn to God. Our personal demise is our greatest possible loss. Job declared, "Our days on earth are like a shadow," and the shadow is not under our control.

A staff is a unique instrument used for the care and management of sheep only. The symbol represents a shepherd's concern and compassion for his sheep. The rod conveys the concept of authority, power, discipline, and defence of the sheep. The staff represents all that is long-suffering and kind.

Psalm 23 reminds us that God is good and worthy of our trust in life or death—times of plenty or want. The psalm uses the metaphor of a shepherd's care for his sheep to describe the wisdom, strength, and kindness of our God.

"The LORD is my shepherd; I shall not want. He makes me lie down in green pastures: he leads me beside the still waters. He restores my soul: he leads me in the paths of righteousness for his name's sake."

Our Shepherd wants to lead us to a place of rest, trust, and confidence, where we can rely on Him and focus on Him without anything distracting us.

So it is with the introspection on the character and life of Biblical characters we can learn great lessons to use in our life for our benefit and those of our fellow man today.

During the days of Jesus' life on earth, he offered up prayers and petitions with loud cries and tears to the one who could save him from death, and he was ultimately heard in God's good time because of hs reverent submission. Although he was a son, in his understanding and link to the Infinite Intelligence, the one he called Father, he learnt obedience.

CHAPTER 4.

JESUS, MIRACLES & SUFFERING.

Many proponents say that for people to escape before this impending judgment on the world and be 'raptured'; they must accept that the 'Christian Messiah' Jesus Christ died for their sins, rose again and is the only means of being reconciled to God. These views are shared by all of the major proponents of the Revelation 21:22 Prophecy. *'But I saw no temple in it, for the Lord God Almighty and the Lamb are its temple. The city has no need of the sun or the moon to shine in it, for the glory of God illuminated it. The lamb is its light.'*

There is a great logical fallacy among Bible sceptics, atheists and those who challenge Christianity that says when discussing historical aspects of the Bible, 'you can't use the Bible as proof that Jesus existed. You use non-Bible sources!' To which this author says ' Well, why not?' The four Gospels of the Bible are bibliographical accounts of the life of Jesus. The normal objective measure of the reliability of historical documents is:1.) the number of available copies of ancient manuscripts. 2.) The period between the original versions and the date of those copies still existing today. The Bible provides proof and evidence that Jesus existed when examined under this standard. All other non-Biblical historicist evidence supports and reinforces this. Manuscript fragments of the New Testament documents, written between 50-100 AD, support all the Biblical and non-Biblical evidence of the existence of Jesus Christ.

The record of the life, ministry, death and resurrection of Jesus Christ has more evidence and proof than any other person from antiquity. Jesus believed that he was just a regular man, but he was reportedly the son of God and gave his life on the cross, so many historians knew about the punishment for the wrongdoings of humanity. It takes faith and trust in that sacrifice to receive him. Jesus said: *['Behold, I stand at the door, and knock: if any man hears my voice and opens the door, I will come into him, and sup with him, and he with me. To him that overcommit will I grant to sit with me in my throne, even as I also overcame and I sit down with my Father in his throne.']* - 'Revelation 3: 20-21.'

Jesus wants us to believe in him based on volumes of documented evidence of his birth, death, Resurrection, and Ascension into heaven. If we are to be free from our defects of character, we have to be committed to our lives here and now to have eternal life in the hereafter and reign with him. So now that it is established that He existed, what is it that he is asking of us? I began to ponder this thought. Still determined to delve further into the matter of faith now and not the evidence of his existence. Did I need to do that, though? What is it that this God of my inner spirit asks of me? I was thinking. In Matthew's gospel, Jesus in the scriptures, particularly the Sermon on the Mount, points out the essence of his teaching: Jesus is consistently seen to be merciful, gracious, faithful, forgiving, and steadfast in love. Of course, living by this Credo is not always easy on a daily basis.

But suppose Jesus is the image of his Father, i.e. the Universal God figure that is nonetheless hard to believe in his existence in the void, and we are called to imitate him. In that case, it stands to reason that the way to live by these principles is to bring those five qualities into play. So, practising mindfulness as Christ dictated in his Sermon on the Mount is to appreciate the need for his grace- that gift that can only be absorbed by doing unto others as they would have us do unto you. Those five qualities of mercy, grace, faith, forgiveness and steadfastness seem to be the catalysts of human action for the betterment of one's self and our fellow man. If that's all there is to it, trying this Christ credo for a better life is worth a shot-being a believer or a nonbeliever. Jesus was only on earth as a man for a short time. Shepherds visited him as a witness to his coming for they had been told already by an angel of his birth. Likewise, Magi Kings had followed a star from the east to the place of his birth, offering gifts of gold, frankincense and myrrh. Apart from his preaching to the priests of the temple at age 12, he goes missing for 18 years and next appears when he returns from 40-day fasting in the desert and is baptised by John the Baptist in the river Jordan. He preached for the next three years to his followers, performed many miracles, predicted future events, and ultimately sacrificed himself on the cross for the wrongdoings of mankind, died and was buried at age 33, rose again from the dead three days later, visited his followers and ascended into the heavens. Jesus not only fulfilled his spoken prophecy in his lifetime, he predicted events that would come to pass some time in the future. One of the ministries was that of a prophet. Jesus had predicted that *'heaven and earth will pass away, but my words will not pass away'* (Mathew 24:35).

To date, his words still echo throughout Christendom, read and believed by untold millions. Mary of Bethany poured oil on Jesus's body in anticipation of his death. The disciples rebuked her for wasting the oil. Jesus chastised them, saying her story would be retold wherever the gospel was preached. This has always come to pass. Jesus also predicted that one of his own would betray him. Judas fulfilled this. Jesus had foreseen that Peter would deny him three times before the cock crowed. This, too, came to pass.

He predicted that he would suffer at the hands of religious rulers. On the night he was arrested, the religious rulers allowed him to be beaten. Jesus foresaw he would die in Jerusalem and upon a cross. Both predictions took place. He predicted that he would die during the Passover and rise again in three days. This is well documented as having occurred, as all his predictions.

Many other events, such as the destruction of the City of Jerusalem within one generation, the destruction of the Temple, the scattering of the Jewish people from their land, their captivity and the ruling of the Holy Land by the Gentiles, the persecution of the Jewish people and though persecuted, the nation of Jews would survive-all of these predictions have been fulfilled. These facts demonstrate beyond any doubt that Jesus was indeed a genuine prophet. During his earthly ministry, Jesus touched and transformed countless lives. Like other events in the life of Jesus, all his miracles were documented by eyewitnesses.

The Gospels record 37 of these and are mentioned in various texts by the four writers Mathew, Mark, Luke and John. The ability at age 12 to interpret holy scriptures and teach wise scribes and priests in the Temple of Jerusalem would seem like a miracle to them at the time. He performed many miracles over the remaining three years before he was crucified. This was followed by healing the sick, casting out evil spirits from the possessed, cleansing those diseased, restoring the use of limbs, restoring the sight of the blind and hearing of the deaf; calming the sea, ensuring a significant fish catch, feeding the multitude, walking on water, bringing people back to life and many more.

Atheists and agnostics who will not accept the Bible as a reference to Christ's existence on this earth and his suffering death on the cross, may be comforted to know that many scholars and scribes outside of the Bible can be relied upon to recount the story of Christ, The first of these was Titus Flavius Josephus (37-c.100), a 1st Century Roman-Jewish historian and hagiographer of priestly ancestry who recorded Jewish history, with particular emphasis on the 1st Century CE and the First Jewish-Roman War, which resulted in the Destruction of Jerusalem and its temple 70 AD. His most important works recount the history of the world from a Jewish perspective for a Roman audience.

These works provide valuable insight into 1st century Judaism and the background of Early Christianity. Josephus was a Jew who did not believe in Jesus Christ as the Son of God or Christianity. In *'The Antiquities of the Jews'*, book 18, chapter 3, paragraph 3 this famous historian writes: [" *Now there was about this time Jesus, a wise man, if it is lawful to call him a man, for he was a doer of wonderful works- a teacher of such men as receive the truth with pleasure. He drew over to him both many of the Jews and many of the Gentiles. He was (the) Christ; and when Pilate, at the suggestion of principal men amongst us, had condemned him to a cross...'*]

Josephus goes on with further proof as to the condemnation of Christ. Josephus, considered one of the greatest historians of antiquity, independently provided proof and evidence of Christ's reality, confirming biblical account. Cornelius Tacitus, a Roman Historian from 55-120 AD, wrote the following passage that refers to Jesus, called 'Christus', which means 'The Messiah', in book 15, chapter 44 of The Annals. After a six-day fire burned much of Rome:['Consequently, to get rid of the report, Nero fastened the guilt and inflicted the most exquisite tortures on a class hated as an abomination, called Christians by the populace. Christus, from whom the name originated, suffered the most extreme of penalties during the reign of Tiberius at the hands of procurator Pontius Pilatus. Titus goes on to describe how the followers of Christ, like him, perished.

Pliny the Younger wrote of the Persecution of Christians. Gaius Plinius Cascilius Secundus (61–112 AD), better known as 'Pliny, The Younger', was a lawyer, author and magistrate of Ancient Rome. He wrote numerous letters to such notables as Tacitus and the Emperor Trajan. He was considered an honest and moderate man, consistent in pursuing suspected Christian members according to Roman law. He rose through a series of Imperial civil and military offices, the 'cursus honorum'- imperial sequential order of office. In correspondence with Emperor Trajan, he reported on his actions against the followers of Christ. He asks the Emperor for instructions dealing with Christians and explains he forced Christians to curse Christ under painful torture. So not only was Pliny aware of Jesus Christ, he also described the activities of the early Church. In later writings, he details persecution against Christians.

Sextus Julius Africanus (c.160.-240 AD) was a Christian traveller and historian of the late 2nd and early 3rd Century AD. He is important chiefly because he influences Eusebius, on all the late writers of the Church history among the Fathers, and on the Greek school of chroniclers. Julius Africanus quotes about writings of Tallus, who was the first non–Christian historian. In his Chronicles, Africanus, quoting the historian Tallus, explains the reason for it being so dark during the time of the day of the crucifixion of Jesus Christ: 'an eclipse of the sun.' non-Christian proof of Jesus' existence and another confirmation of the Bible's accounts of Jesus' crucifixion."

Lucian (Born 115AD) was a well-known Greek satirist and a travelling lecturer. More than eighty works bear his name. He mocked Christians in his writing, but at the same time, provided evidence that Jesus was real. 'He was second only to that one whom they worship today, the man in Palestine who was crucified because he brought this new form of initiation into the world.' He goes on to describe the beliefs of Christians, the personal sacrifices they make, and their transgression from denying Greek Gods to worship of this Christian God. The Christa were all on one level with this God in their belief for eternity. Lucian does not mention Christ by name, but he confirms his existence that he was crucified in 'Palestine', had followers who believed in eternal life and that they were equal to Jesus Christ.

Lucian even mentions that Christians deny all other gods and believe in 'faith alone.'This, again is in keeping with the Bible's clear statements about the Christian faith and provides more evidence of the existence of Christ that 'the man in Palestine, did exist.' Gaius Suetonius Tranquillus, known as Suetonius (circa 69-75 AD) was a Roman historian from the equestrian order era in the early Imperial era. His most important surviving work is a set of biographies of twelve successive Roman rulers from Julius Caesar to Domitian, entitled *'De Vita Caesarum'*. In the apparent description of his writing, he states Emperor Claudius reigned from 41AD to 524 AD.' Suetonius reports his dealings with the eastern Roman Empire, that is, Greece and Macedonia, and with Lycian, Rhodesians, and Trojans. He then reports that the Emperor expelled Jews from Rome since they 'constantly made disturbances at the instigation of Christ.'

All other non-biblical historicist evidence supports and reinforces this. Manuscript fragments of the New Testament documents, written between 50 and 100 AD, support all the biblical and non-biblical evidence of Jesus Christ's existence.

The record of the life, ministry, death and resurrection of Jesus Christ has more evidence and proof than any other person from antiquity. Jesus believed that he was just a regular man, but he was reportedly the son of God and gave his life on the cross so many historians knew about the punishment for the wrongdoings of humanity. It takes faith and trust in that sacrifice to receive him.

To date, his words still echo throughout Christendom, read and believed by untold millions. Mary of Bethany poured oil on the body of Jesus in her anticipation of his death. She was rebuked by the disciples for wasting the oil. Jesus chastised them saying that her story would be retold wherever the gospel was preached. This has always come to pass.

Jesus also predicted that one of his own would betray him. This was literally fulfilled by Judas. Jesus had foreseen that Peter would deny him three times before the cock crowed. This too came to pass. He predicted that he would suffer at the hands of religious rulers. On the night he was arrested the religious rulers allowed him to be beaten. Jesus foresaw he would die in Jerusalem and upon a cross. Both predictions took place. He predicted that he would die during the Passover and would rise again in three days. This is well documented as having occurred as were all of his predictions.

We are to understand that God that God came to earth in the incarnate Jesus who was recognised as being "Full of Grace." God came as a man. Jesus identified with men living life side by side with humanity. " He had to be made like his brothers in every way, in order that he might become merciful and faithful as a high priest in the services of God, and that he might make atonement for the sins of the people. Because he himself suffered when he was tempted , he is able to help those who are being tempted too.

The writers of Hebrew speaks of Jesus being 'made perfect' through suffering: " In bringing many sons to glory. It was fitting that God, for whom and through whom everything exists, should make the author of their salvation perfect through suffering. Jesus suffering was essential, in some way, for the divine plan of salvation. In Fact Hebrew speaks of Jesus, that even though he was the Son of God incarnate, he suffered as a man as a type of learning experience in his earthly life.

For Christians suffering plays a vital role in the life and ministry of Jesus, our Saviour. Scripture make it clear that Jesus suffered throughout his life and not just during his Passion and death on the cross. If we take it that he was ever present as a part of the nature of God from the very beginning, then he suffered the loss of his eternal standing in heaven when he accepted and entered the the nature of man on earth. (Phil. 2.5:11). On many occasions during his earthly ministry he faced scorn, ridicule, doubt, and outright opposition from those who either did not understand him or who understood him all too well.

He suffered every hardship and all the while Satan and his minions temptation where inflicted upon him. Jesus took absorbed and suffered the pains of every person he healed. He suffered the lack of comforts and conveniences. Jesus had nowhere he called home or a place where he could lay his head. He was rejected by those of his own community too. He suffered the harassment of people who insisted that he minister on their schedule rather than his own. He suffered disciples, slow to understand, who never quite got it, but, he knew one day they would. Amid of all his suffering Jesus never once appealed to the world for relief. He did not complain about his suffering. It seems that we are meant to emulate him, to be drawn to this Jesus figure, the 'man of sorrows' in our times of great need and suffering be that mental, physical or spiritual. It not so easy to lean in a little to our suffering selves and contemplate the nature of suffering for our betterment. This Jesus accepted humiliation as suffering servant for all-an incarnate deity, his suffered the passion, death, burial, decent into Hades and ascended into the heavens, as an atonement for the wrongs we do through our defects of character.

We have, apart from Christ's whom Paul writes " God made him who had no sin to be the burden of our sin for us." In returning to the fact that Jesus was made perfect, it indicated that he was fully qualified to be saviour of mankind undergoing the experience of human suffering, since suffering is the way to salvation. It is written that Jesus did not display the normal traits of defects of character that the rest of humanity did and still does. Except maybe on one occasion when he took off the cord from his waist and angrily whipped the money traders in the entry to the temple exclaiming' " My house is a hose of prayer but you have made it a den of thieves." It was justifiable anger for one who could see his destiny clearly.

In nature we see through its history repeated period of great suffering. The world itself suffers to this day with volcanic eruptions, devastation tornadoes creating the destructive force of violently rotating winds, tidal waves bringing havoc to nature and man. Floods, fire and drought are everyday experiences in our world.

In examining nature there is much suffering in ever changing conditions. A simple seed planted in the earth by nature or man must endure a period of suffering as it breaks through the crust and crud of the earth to ultimately bloom as a flower. Animals in an evolutionary cycle and pecking order suffer to eat and are killed by prey of a higher species for their survival too. Nature is both cruel and kind and man, like nature and the animals must learn to have acceptance to his own nature and the natur-al, order or chaos that surround him in every day existence.

We must learn to embrace suffering as we are taught from our very beginning on this earth to do. At birth a baby passing through the birth canal suffers greatly before we hear its first cry. It is not only a difficult experience for a mother to give birth it is proven that the child being born suffers the greater pain.

When we suffer greatly though tragedy with the loss of a love one, experience a broken relationships, or indeed lose earthly possessions, lose a career, or suffer the pain of ill health or be-come involved with another misfortune, it is hard to accept. Given time however all things pass for the better and its al-ways a learning experience. So much more for the embracing of suffering with Christ as our guiding light..

Our suffering it is gaining the importance of what to make of it in our life. What we make of it in terms of how to understand it, and in terms of hoe we allow it to affect us. Here is where theology helps; it allow us to see suffering in a positive light, as a means of growth rather than as something meaningless. We can offer our sufferings and distress to God, assured that he can and will use them to bring us to new depth of faith and service.

Whatever the cause or occasion of such suffering, God means to address his children in that very place, and to use that expe-rience to make us more like Christ. When we have our ladder of daily living firmly up against a wall according to out will and not Gods he cant get it. We may suffer much as a conse-quence of living in the ego and the result is meaningless.

In setting our goals towards God's will and not our own we come to terms with suffering in a mature way. If suffering was the means by which the sinless Christ became mature, so much more do we need it in our defects of character actions. Just as suffering led to maturity through obedience for Christ, so to Christ leads us to maturity through his perseverance for us.

Jesus said: "I came that they may have life, and may have it abundantly. ... The thief cometh not, but to steal, and to kill, and to destroy: I am come that they may have life and have it abundantly. "

Abundance doesn't come from attaining material things, purchasing investments, or even achieving goals. The secret to living an abundant life is contentment. Contentment makes you feel rich regardless of your circumstances. Whether you have a lot of money or a little, contentment turns it into enough.It is living through the suffering that man finds the road to freedom life in abundance with God.

CHAPTER 5.

PETER THE ROCK

According to the apocryphal Acts of Peter, the disciple Peter's martyrdom should have been a moment of great suffering. He was arrested and crucified during the reign of the Roman Emperor Nero, possibly during one of the early purges of those Christians living in Rome. In this legendary tradition, Peter is said to have attempted to flee from Rome to escape persecution before encountering a vision of Jesus on the Via Appia that stunned him by simply asking him, 'Quo Vadis?', or 'Where are you going?' Jesus was, he had said, going into Rome to be crucified again, a statement that apparently and dramatically stopped Peter from fleeing and prompted him to accept his destiny, to return to Rome and be subject to crucifixion himself. The encounter describes how the followers of Christ, like him, perished. They bore enough symbolic gravity that Jesus' feet were allegedly pressed into the stone beneath him, an image preserved at San Sebastian outside the walls of a nearby church.

After Peter's arrest, and just before he was exposed to the means that would bring about his death, Peter is said to have asked his executioners to let him experience his being crucifiied upside down, as he did not feel worthy to die in the same manner as Jesus had—a sign of his humility, but also his acceptance of the situation. Peter's reception of his martyrdom, in the face of much suffering in cited upon both himself and many other early Christians in the nascent Church—indeed, these were the believers upon whom some of the most horrific cruelty was inflicted.

Peter's death perhaps somewhat resonated with Paul's claim in Acts that his life was 'worth nothing' to him, his 'only aim' being 'to finish the race and complete the task the Lord Jesus has given me—the task of testifying to the good news of God's grace' (Acts 20:24), something that takes place without necessarily a consideration of the suffering that one might.

Lest we forget, Paul is the one who counsels his fellow Christians by boasting of his suffering (Corinthians 2 11.16-33) and by rejoicing in it because it produces perseverance, character and ultimately hope (Romans 5.3-10). Paul was no stranger to suffering, and we might suspect that Peter was no stranger to it at this point in his life. But what are we to make of Peter's suffering when he was crucified in comparison to what he felt when he denied Jesus? What kind of suffering did he experience in this denial? I want to ask about Peter's suffering after he denied Christ three times: How does this suffering measure or clarify the daily suffering many of us feel?

The story of Peter's denial is familiar enough: they seized him and led him away, bringing him into the high priest's house. But Peter was following at a distance. When they had kindled a fire in the middle of the courtyard and sat down together, Peter sat among them. Then a servant-girl, seeing him in the firelight, stared at him and said, "This man also was with him." But he denied it, saying, "Woman, I do not know him."
Then, about an hour later, another kept insisting, "Surely this man also was with him, for he is a Galilean." But Peter said, "Man, I do not know what you are talking about!" At that moment, while he was still speaking, the cock crowed. The Lord turned and looked at Peter. Then Peter remembered the word of the Lord, how he had said to him, "Before the cock crows today, you will deny me three times."

We recall Peter had been willing to go to battle for Christ, even to die for Christ. He brought his sword to the fight in the garden and even cut off a soldier's ear in an act of defensive aggression. He made abundantly clear that he was ready to suffer significantly on behalf of a cause (perhaps understood as one undertaken for social, political and religious freedom), and so in Christ's defence. He might even have considered himself not suffering at all but fully immersed in an act of potential martyrdom, hence not so much suffering, as being honoured to die for something that meant a good deal to him. (One might imagine here the many causes and protests that Christians sometimes take up because they feel a social or political injustice is being done to them—often embraced as a valiant effort in a particular context's 'culture wars'—though it is not something that arises out of a sense of solidarity with those others who are sick or suffering.)

In this sense, we have an uneasy parallel between Peter's willingness to die in the garden fighting for Christ and his actual death through crucifixion while also undergoing another sort of 'struggle' for Christ. At points throughout history, as one can imagine, there has been an inevitable overlap between the stories and languages of peaceful martyrdom and that of militant warrior. Though there may be a great distinction between them in terms of their relationship to violent action, there may also be a strong similarity in terms of there rejecting a discourse of suffering to describe what they undergo. The question we have to ask, then, concerns the point at which Peter was one of the 12 Apostles of Jesus. Roman Catholic tradition holds that Jesus established St. Peter as the first pope (Matthew 16:18). Jesus also gave him "the keys of the kingdom of heaven" (Matthew 16:19), which is why he is often depicted at the gates of heaven in art and popular culture. genuine suffering takes place in Peter's life, but which seems at a certain remove from all the fighting and death—the point at which he breaks down and weeps bitterly.

The suffering accompanies an inevitable disillusionment. Perhaps the situation that arose was, in some strange way, the suffering that Christ asked Peter to undergo and that which
Jesus had foreseen as bound up with the future of a man who had so frequently misunderstood the nature of Jesus' mission and teaching. misunderstood the nature of Jesus' mission and teaching. For years, Peter had miscalculated the nature of Jesus' messianic proclamation, expecting a military and revolutionary leader instead of what he had before his eyes. The hopes that legions of angel armies might descend upon ancient Palestine to remove Roman occupation, for example—was shattered when the centrepiece of their political aspirations was killed like a common criminal.

At this point, Peter could genuinely say that he didn't know Jesus, that he didn't know the man he had thought he knew because he didn't know him in a certain sense—a fact that adds an ironic twist to Peter's denials of Christ. But Jesus had already seen this coming: to so wilfully misunderstand Jesus' mission for so long could only lead to disillusionment and desertion once the realisation of Jesus' all-too-obvious 'weakness' hit home. It was at this precise moment, however, that Jesus asked Peter to face himself, to look deeper into his motives and an inner path toward a transformation that Peter had already failed time and again to grasp.

On the mountaintop where Jesus was transfigured before his eyes, Peter had misunderstood what was happening, offering to build three booths for Jesus, Moses and Elijah, missing the point of Jesus' becoming as radiant as Moses had been on top of Mount Sinai when he had received the Law from God. Peter had missed that this wasn't a moment that foreshadowed the coming new Law—instead, the Law was now standing before him, was in Peter's very presence, and he could not recognise it for what it was. Since Peter had denied Christ three times, the Lord only turned to look at him. Only when Peter had admitted to himself that he was broken and that the illusions he had fostered about Jesus had not been what he had so badly wanted them to be did the space of vulnerability open up within him that could allow the presence of God to find him. This point indeed underlies the life of prayer and intimacy that Christians seek to cultivate in their spiritual lives.

Only after facing the suffering that he had brought upon himself and in his disillusionment with how his constructed life had failed to achieve what he had sought so desperately to claim for himself, is Peter able to face other forms of suffering that he once might have thought he could not handle, ones where a sword would do him no good. Indeed, once Peter has faced his brokenness, he has no use for the sword, which would only serve to re-inscribe him to the struggles for power that have no place within God's Kingdom.

What Peter discovered, I think, is that it is in such moments of suffering, of bitter tears, that we are most capable of glimpsing the face of God. Peter sees God, who turned to look directly at him once he had seen his failure to indeed suffer on behalf of Jesus, to stand at the foot of the cross and to risk his life (as the beloved disciple, perhaps an idealised type, had done, and as indeed the women following him had done). It is only at this point, after being willing to suffer the loss of his illusions, that Peter can go out from the crowd, stand alone, and in this solitude, weep bitterly. At a time when many of us are facing a sense of isolation and alienation

The suffering and bitterness that we are told about seem to be far more significant and more believable than either the possible suffering in the garden on behalf of a false idea of Jesus or the martyrdom on Jesus' behalf that can be borne only because there is nothing left to fight for—the transfiguration and transformation through suffering had already taken place.

From Peter's perspective, it is only once he faces his brokenness, after he weeps bitterly, that he can put down the sword and work for mercy in the lives of others; even up to the point of his death. The Christian martyr defined society, while the political revolutionary might only reinforce another, different image. Peter had made the remarkable journey from the latter to the former and was willing to lay down his life for those less fortunate. The suffering felt in his brokenness had gained him access to his soul's purpose.

Peter is one of Scripture's most endearing characters. There's just something dynamic about his personality. It's so easy to identify with him because he's so utterly human. We see him opening his mouth at inappropriate times and saying outlandish things. One minute you'll find him promising undying devotion to Jesus, and the next he's standing in a courtyard swearing he's never even heard of Jesus.

Despite being overzealous and impulsive, that's probably what makes Jesus pull this disciple into His inner circle. Along with James and John, Peter shares an intimacy with Jesus that the other disciples don't experience. Luke gives us an in-depth glimpse into Peter's calling. Jesus showed up on the shore of Galilee, climbed into a boat, and asked to be rowed out so He could teach the crowd. It just so happens that the boat He chose belonged to Peter. After teaching for a while, Jesus told Peter to take them into deep water and drop the nets. Peter scoffed. They'd been working all night, and they hadn't caught anything-but he did as he was told.

When they had done so, they caught such a large number of fish that their nets began to break. So they singled their partners in the other boat to come and help them, and they came and filled both boats so full that they began to sink.

When Simon Peter saw this, he fell at Jesus' knees and said, 'Go away from me, Lord; I am a sinful man!'" (Luke 5:6-8) The way Jesus handles the situation is touching: "When they had finished eating, Jesus said to Simon Peter, 'Simon son of John, do you love me more than these?

'Yes, Lord,' he said, 'you know that I love you.'
Jesus said, 'Feed my lambs.'
Again Jesus said, 'Simon son of John, do you love me?'
He answered, 'Yes, Lord, you know that I love you.'
Jesus said, 'Take care of my sheep.'
The third time he said to him, 'Simon son of John, do you love me?' Peter was hurt because Jesus asked him the third time, 'Do you love me?' He said, 'Lord, you know all things; you know that I love you.'
Jesus said, 'Feed my sheep'" (John 21:15-17).

Peter learns to be courageous, he overcomes his fear and cowardliness and becomes the first evangelist in preaching the word that Jesus taught him. Peter comforts Gentile Christians who were suffering under Roman oppression by reassuring them of their identity and purpose. Suffering injustice can feel like evidence of defeat, but Peter reminds the people of the victory Jesus accomplished through suffering. While many more things could be said to explain Peter's prominence among Christ's Apostles, the points outlined above compel us to focus on a common theme: the brokenness of the man, his redemption and transformation that comes by faith in the risen Lord Jesus Christ despite his own weakness.

CHAPTER 6.

PAUL THE EVANGELIST

Before his conversion, Paul was known as Saul and was "a Pharisee of Pharisees, who "intensely persecuted" the powers of Jesus. Paul describes his life before conversion in his Epistle to the Galatians.

["For you have heard of my previous way of life in Judaism, how intensely I persecuted the church of God and tried to destroy it. I was advancing in Judaism beyond many of my own age among my people and was extremely zealous for the traditions of my fathers. As he neared Damascus on his journey, suddenly a light from heaven flashed around him. He fell to the ground and heard a voice say to him, "Saul, Saul, why do you persecute me?" "Who are you, Lord?" Saul asked. "I am Jesus, whom you are persecuting," he replied.]

The men traveling with Saul stood there speechless; they heard the sound but did not see anyone. Paul got up from the ground, but when he opened his eyes he could see nothing. So they led him by the hand into a house in Damascus. For three days he was blind, and did not eat or drink anything. (Acts 9:3-9) Ananias, a local follower of Jesus, a pious man, while initially fearful, finds the blinded Paul and greets him as a brother. Ananias lays his hands on Paul, and the apostle's sight is restored as something like scales fall from his eyes. Paul is immediately baptised, and the church's great enemy becomes its great advocate.

The conversion of Paul the Apostle was, according to the New Testament, an event in the life of Saul/Paul the apostle that caused him to cease persecuting early Christians and become a follower of Jesus.

The lesson is that the power coms from God; the person is the vessel. When God calls a person to a task, he equips that person for it. Paul received the Holy Spirit, along with the truth of the gospel so he could share it with others. Paul could not have achieved this remarkable accomplishment of his own strength-.without the support of God. In the Pauline epistles, the description of Paul's conversion experience is brief. In the First Epistle to the Corinthians 9:2 and 15:3-8 describes Paul as having seen the risen Christ.

He later writes "For what I received I passed on to you as of first importance: that Christ died for our sins according to the Scriptures, that he was buried, that he was raised on the third day according to the Scriptures, and that he appeared to Cephas, and then to the Twelve. After that, he appeared to more than five hundred of the brothers and sisters at the same time, most of whom are still living, though some have fallen asleep. Then he appeared to James, then to all the apostles, and last of all he appeared to me also, as to one abnormally born.'—1 Corinthians 15:3–8,

Despite his previous beliefs as a Pharisee, he now knew the truth about God and was obligated to obey him. Paul's conversion proves that God can call and transform anyone he soever chooses, even the most hard- hearted. God chose Saul to be His instrument to share the Good News with the Gentiles. We learn that God has a purpose and plan for each person that places his/her faith in Jesus.

Paul explains his acceptance his lot and in his zeal explains his purposes in preaching the importance of embracing the Lord and doing his will not his own. "It is necessary to boast; nothing is to be gained by it, but I will go on to visions and revelations of the Lord. I know a person in Christ who fourteen years ago was caught up to the third heaven—whether in the body or out of the body I do not know; God knows. And I know that such a person—whether in the body or out of the body I do not know; God knows— was caught up into Paradise and heard things that are not to be told, that no mortal is permitted to repeat. On behalf of such a one I will boast, but on my own behalf I will not boast, except of my weaknesses. But if I wish to boast, I will not be a fool, for I will be speaking the truth. But I refrain from it, so that no one may think better of me than what is seen in me or heard from me, even considering the exceptional character of the revelations. Therefore, to keep me from being too elated, a thorn was given me in the flesh, a messenger of Satan to torment me, to keep me from being too elated."

He goes on to relate where his message is derived: "I want you to know, brothers and sisters, that the gospel I preached is not of human origin. I did not receive it from any man, nor was I taught it; rather, I received it by revelation from Jesus Christ. For you have heard of my previous way of life in Judaism, how intensely I persecuted the church of God and tried to destroy it. [...] But when God, who set me apart from my mother's womb and called me by his grace, was pleased to reveal his Son in me so that I might preach him among the Gentiles, my immediate response was not to consult any human being."

The apostle Paul was no stranger to suffering in his zeal to preach the Gospel of Jesus, the saviour. He describes his hardship in a letter to the Corinthians, listing troubles and disr tress of various kinds, including beatings, imprisonments, riots, hard work, sleepless flights, and hunger. Later in the same

letter Paul boasts about his sufferings in comparison to others :
" I have worked much harder, been in prison more frequently,
been flogged mote severely, and been exposed to death again
and again. Five times I received from the Jews the forty
lashes minus one. Three times I was beaten with rods, once I
was stoned, three times I was shipwrecked. I spent a night and
a day in the open sea. I have been constantly on the move. I
have been in danger crossing swollen rivers, in danger by
bandits, in danger from my own countrymen, in danger of the
gentiles, in danger in the city, in danger in the country, in danger at sea; and in danger from false brothers. I have laboured
and toiled and gone without sleep, I have known hunger and
thirst and often gone without food, I have been cold and
naked."

Suffering for Paul was no abstract question, it was his daily
life. This evoked a pressing question fro Paul; the question of
why Christians, who already begun to experience the powers
of the age to come, should be subjected more affliction than
others. And there was also the question of why Paul, a faithful
apostle of the Lord Jesus should have such an abundance of
suffering in his own life and ministry. Suffering fro Paul was a
way of identifying with Christ. The sense of identification with
the sufferings of Christ, as well as the victory of Christ, became for Paul the foundation of the practical response to his
suffering. For like Jesus, Paul learned genuineness through
suffering… the experience of ' always being given over to
death for Jesus' sake. (Cor. 4:11) freed him from having to insist on his rights: what right does an executed victim have? He
is also free to be real: what need is there too for phoniness if
one is about to die?' The prospect of Paul's imminent death
caused Paul to rely not on himself but on God. Through his
experience of a thorn in the flesh, described in 2 Corinthians
12:-7, Paul gained a deeper understanding about false and

true ways of self fulfilment. His troubles drew him to other people, both fro the sake of consoling them with God's truth and for him to find solace in their company.

Paul describes his struggle against mistakes due to defects of character in Romans 7:14-25. Be it the standpoint of his own experiences in this struggle with his own mistakes, sickness or hardship and afflictions that accompanied his ministry, suffering s central to his life. " I die every day" her says in 1 Corinthians 15:31 he was among those who always carried around in their body, mind and spirit the death of Jesus. The the main explanation from Paul's suffering, is for Christ's sake is found in its effect on other believers and their relationship to god. Paul says: "So then, death is at work in us. But life is at work in you."

Paul's goal was not to avoid suffering but rather to know it. In the letter to the church of Colossal he wrote: "Now I rejoice in what we suffered for you, and I fill up in my flesh what is still lacking in regard to Christ's afflictions, fro the sake of his body, which is the church; a communion brought about by the "convocation-of the assembly of the people " in Christ, is the Church. The suffering Paul wants to know is the suffering of Christ. " I want to know Christ and power of the resurrection and the fellowship of his sufferings, becoming like him in his death, and so, somehow, to attain to the resurrection from the dead," Paul knows that it is the partnership with Christ's Suffering that suffering fulfils a redemptive purpose and gains a resurrection perspective.

Paul's pursuit of Christ's suffering was not due to the fact that Christ gave Paul and other believers an appetite for suffering.It is Christ whop actually shares in Paul's suffering. Paul considers his suffering to be much more valuable than anything he could secure in the flesh. For Paul, the fellowship of sharing in Christ's suffering is priceless, far outweighing any security he might find in the flesh. For Paul to gain what Christ offers cannot be capitalised on without accepting the same loss as Christ did.

In regard to his minister, Paul understood his approval by God to be connected to his willingness to suffer. He refers to struggles he faced and how he preached the gospel " in spite of strong opposition." Near the end of his life, Paul's closing remarks issued a reminder to Timothy of the apostle's view." For I am already being poured out like a drink offering and the time has come for me to depart. I have fought the good fight, i have finished the race, I have kept the faith." Fighting the fight and finishing the race are two athletic metaphors use d by Paul to reveal his life full of struggles and he strains forward towards God's call in Christ. He also spoke of having been tested by God and of being in a position of receiving God's approval (1 Thessalonians 2:4). Although he doesn't call this testing "suffering" he does write of it almost immediately after writing about his preaching of the word in the face of opposition.(1 Thessalonians 1.2:2). There is no great leap to connect Paul's reference to capacity for struggle with God's testing of and approval of him.

There is a connection with Paul's willingness to suffer for the sake of the gospel to his thinking about his own sanctification. In 1 Thessalonians, Paul unites his righteous and blameless behaviour with the willingness to extend himself beyond the norm for the sake of the followers of Christ. He sees his sanctity manifest in his capacity to accept hardship for the sake of others, thereby intimating that he may have interpreted his afflictions as necessary for his growth towards God.

Paul does not address whether or not suffering contributes to growth in holiness for other believers of Christ. Paul as saying of his own hardships in preaching the gospel are part of what brought him divine approval, but he stops short of acknowledging the same relates to other believers suffering to the benefit of their own commendable holiness. Paul is by occupation a tent maker and used the symbolism of his holiness is a the needle through which the threads of faith, hope and love are threaded. Through the Thessalonians to whom Paul preached came people who exhibited faith, hope and love and who also suffer with their faith, hope and love expressed through their suffering. "Paul does not say that his growth in perfection requires his suffering. He says rather his growth in perfection requires his striving."

Paul's own example was the righteous suffer who strove for the upward call of god. The mist significant point in Paul's thesis is that his striving was as one seized by Christ. "I press on to take hold of that which Christ Jesus took hold of me." Suffering is part and parcel of Paul's constituted efforts in growing towards holiness. Paul interprets his suffering as identification with Christ crucified. His suffering must be perpetual, for suffering is requisite for the divine power.

The doctrine of Christian suffering is no mistake in the lives of followers of Christ, the man of sorrows and his passion, death and ultimate resurrection. The most important thing to recognise in Pau's evangelistic preaching is the acceptance of suffering for Godly purpose. It is what we now make of it,
both in terms of how we understand suffering and how we allow it to affect us. Here is where the the study of nature of God

and indeed what Paul preached and demonstrated by his life, come into play.

The nature of God and religious belief allows us to offer our sufferings and distress to God, assured that he can and will use them to bring us to new depths of faith and service. Whatever the cause or occasion of suffering, God means to address his children in that very place, and to use that experience to make them more Christ-like. If suffering was the means by which a divine pure man without our defects of character-Christ became mature, so much more do we need it in our defective nature. Just as suffering led to maturity Paul through obedience to Christ, so it leads us to maturity through perseverance too.

CHAPTER 7.

BEING PATIENT IN SUFFERING

Suffering is a universal human experience. A person cannot go through life without encountering moments that cause grief and pain and despair, the ingredients that make up the suffering experience. The genesis of that suffering - of the presence of evil in the world - has been one of the central questions of Christian theology since the earliest days of the church. Does God allow the existence of suffering, in order to teach humanity a lesson, or build character, or as a means of weeding out the weak and undeserving? Or, perhaps, did God step back from Creation, as a clockmaker would after winding his device, and leave it to its (and our) own devices, which means the finite nature of humanity leaves room for mistake and hurt?

What is in our view, however, are the implications of how humanity understands the mechanism of suffering, and what it means for interactions among groups of people. Most reasoning humans, particularly if they have a faith in God, tend to understand and accept that pain and suffering are part and parcel with being human. That there is an element of pain and suffering in living the very day life.

However, it's a different story in the mind and every day living of those of us who suffer alcoholism. It feels like we are singled out to feel suffering more acutely than most. We ultimately wake up to then face that we are square pegs trying to fit into round holes. Until we ceased drinking and stay sober a day at a time we are prone to use alcohol as an elixir to take charge over our very being. Under the influence of this fluid we escape into a world where pain and suffering are blocked out and we no longer need to accept reality. It is as if we are free whilst we booze, but as is always the case we cause much pain and heartache to others and ourselves. We are a constant train wreck in the making whenever we hit the booze and ultimately we crash and burn. Alcohol becomes our master and we just can't live without it. We find we can't stop drinking. One drink is too many and a thousand not enough. Beaten and worn by our excesses we, with luck, retreat to the entry doors of Alcoholic Anonymous as the last bastion of hope to beat the booze and overcome our pain and suffering.

When we take take the first step in AA, we realise we are powerless over alcohol and ultimately that we are powerless over people, places and everyday things. Thus, when we are on the road to recovery, a day at a time, we come to believe in a power greater than self. The programme teaches us to do the suggested steps of recovery back to sanity and we wake up to the fact that there is a power greater than ourselves who runs the show. That one is God, that we may embrace as the one of our own understanding.

Whist we may stray far from this godliness in living according to our own will, we come to be aware, particularly for alcoholics, that we are square pegs trying to fit into round holes. It is like try as we may despite the fact that we may doing everything to avoid suffering, attempting to live to our egotistical notions which will ultimately be detriment to our soul- that place that love is granted through the surrendering to a Higher Power. We Alcholics learn the pathway to surrender to God as our only means of coping with our disease and in the company of our fellow members learn to share our sufferings with one another and in turn help those who still suffer down the pathway to rack and ruin whilst continuing to drink.

It seems through historic documents and ancient biblical scrolls that Jesus as a man was inspired to take up the cross to save mankind from the wrath that God the father (his and ours) might rain down upon future generations. This is evident by the stories that unfolded from the Old Testament. It appears that God infused in Jesus the man the perfection of the spiritual link to the spirit of love, in that by accepting his suffering throughout his life time and the ultimate death on the cross we have a spiritual link to a spiritual third person in the Godhead-that of a Holy Spirit (or higher self) This gives us the acceptance of suffering and to have the courage and will of God in this our new way of the spiritual journey.

Jesus found it difficult to accept the will of the Father over his own will: In Luke 22:41 he prayed to the Father. "If you are willing, let this cup pass from me. Yet not my will, but thine be done." This provides for us a perfect pray to the surrender of our own will to God Almighty, or for Christians through Christ as the second person of the Trinity of Father, Son and Holy Spirit.

What did Jesus relate then to his followers: again in Luke 9:23:24 he said to them all: "Whoever wants to be my disciple must deny themselves and take up their cross daily and follow me. For whoever wants to save their life will lose it, but whoever loses their life for me will save it. For we can now see that Jesus deliberately surrender himself to the cross, as did Peter and Paul as told in previous chapters. We may have distanced ourselves from Him because of shame, pain, confusion, or disappointment but it appeared that we will be saved if we but take up our burdens and use our talents through Jesus' guidance in Christian doctrine and in the case of alcoholics by following the suggested steps of the AA programme.

For Atheists and Agnostics with a substance use disorder, the "God issue" can be a major barrier that prevents them from seeking treatment in a 12-step program. It is undeniable that Christianity has influenced this form of treatment. After all, the 4th Edition of the Big Book iterates the word "God" 330 times. This does not mean are in any way exclusive though. Many atheists and agnostics find comfort in the programs, and they find a way around the verbiage used in 12-Step literature. If you are wondering whether you can fully embrace a twelve-step program as an atheist, read on to find guidance.

Before Narcotics Anonymous, Cocaine Anonymous, Heroin Anonymous, and many other addiction treatment programmes, there was Alcoholics Anonymous (AA). AA was founded in 1935. Bill Wilson, also known as Bill W., is the first person people think of when it comes to important figureheads in 12-step programs.

What many people don't know is that there were atheists and agnostics in the First AA groups. Some of their experiences are told in the book *Biographies of the Authors of the Stories in the Big Book* compiled by Nancy Moyer Olson. The two main agnostic and atheists who helped found the AA organisation were Jim Burwell and Hank Parkhurst.

Though only two co-founders are officially recognised, many people consider Jim Burwell, also known as Jim B., to be the third founder of AA. He was a member of the New York AA community who advanced to number 4 in the hierarchy. He fought aggressively against the use of God during the meetings. He was a staunch atheist, and he recognised that the overwhelming religiosity of the group would isolate recovering individuals who didn't ascribe to Christianity.

Hank Parkhurst, also known as Hank P., is an unsung hero of AA. Though Hank was the second person to stay sober for any long period of time in the New York AA group, his existence within the Big Book has largely been scrubbed. The chapter he wrote was not attributed to him and he is only mentioned in veiled references. Hank P. was an agnostic member of AA who was uncomfortable with how often "God" appeared in the original 12 steps.

As the Big Book was developed, he helped Jim B.and Hank P. refused to sign the 12-steps document until it was edited to be more inclusive. They wanted it to omit references to God altogether. Eventually, everyone compromised. They added a sentence emphasising the steps' position as guidance instead of rules. They added "as we understood Him" as a qualifier to any mention of God. Jim B. and Hank P. insisted on changing the verbiage to reference a higher power.

Secular atheists have come to reference themselves as "friends of Jim B." instead of "friends of Bill W." As an atheist considering a 12-step program, try to remember that these two men fought for your right to be in the sober community. You have a place in any 12-step program whether other members think so or not.

Now that you understand the background of atheists and agnostics in 12-step, you are hopefully feeling more welcome. Still, the issue of constantly referencing to a higher power may put off many never the less found alternatives to remain in the programme. I fully sympathise with the agnostics and the atheist in being in AA and being faced with the religious zeal of some members in expressing their views of the need for a god head to lean upon to remain sober and carry the message of AA steps. Whilst I myself was brought up Catholic and indoctrinated with the Catechism as the instruction of belief of Christianity, I never the less lost my way in adulthood. The logical linear half brain notion of what God was all about allowed me the luxury of living a kind of moral coexistence with worldly values. It seem to work fine living with the Godhead on one shoulder and a Protestant work ethic on the other. Ultimately that failed me too when a series of tragic circumstances engulfed me.

I found no answers to my dilemma in falling down the well of loss of confidence in God and in humanity at large. There seemed to be no way out and alcohol became my only friend for a time. I was already on the downward spiral intro full blown alcoholism before the rot set in; drink was my bandaid to get me through the day. Ultimately, I became highly addicted and I found myself in rehab and unable to drink again. It was via a suggestion by a fellow patient in rehab that I turned to AA for help. I had nowhere else to turn and thank God I did.

In time I learnt to accept a power greater than self was the only road to recovery fro me mentally, physically and spiritually. I learnt to live by the power of the creative imagination and to escape the logical viewpoint of a God. I created a manifestation of what I perceived God to be for me. This worked for a number of years in sobriety but ultimately I had to face the reality of it all; look at God as both being two sides of my brain power, that of the linear brain and that of the creative one. The symbols and signs of the 'faith of my fathers holy faith' began to draw me back to my indoctrinated belief as equally as the manifested belief of my creative self will and the influences of AA.

In some cases a black and white view of AA fellowship itself as a 12 Step fellowship gives meaning too many atheists and agnostics and they remain sober with this method of belief. Others use a psychological approach, relying on conscious efforts and their efforts in the community at large as their way of remaining sober- applying th steps to their daily living this way. In more recent times, attempting to define my belief in a Higher power I've taken to refer to the God head as an Infinite Intelligence that made all and runs the universe and everything in it.

If you can't get past the constant references to God or higher powers, then consider this. Some allude to spirituality more vaguely. Some only reference a higher power as something outside of our control. Some are catered for specifically to one religion. If a person has embraced some form of the 12-steps, it may be easier for them to attend a program based on this religious structure. After all, the first six steps of the AA programme originated from a Christian plan of action of a prayer group at Oxford in the early 20th century based on the principles of self improvement by performing self inventory, admitting wrongs, making amends, using prayer and meditation, and carrying the message to others.

Plus, no matter which version of the 12-steps is selected, atheists can gain comfort from the fact that there is diversity with the community. As Tradition Three of Alcoholics Anonymous states, 'Our membership ought to include all who suffer from alcoholism.' "Hence we may refuse none who wish to recover. Nor ought AA membership ever depend upon money or conformity. Any two or three alcoholics gathered together for sobriety may call themselves an AA group, provided that, as a group, they have no other affiliation."

All 12-step programs need to create an inclusive space for people with different religious values and beliefs. This is especially true because, when they participate, 12-step programs are just as effective fro atheists as for theists.

As it says in a daily reflection in the Big Book of AA, page 87: "Being still inexperienced and having just made conscious contact with God (or what we may perceive God to be-) it is not probable that we are going to be inspired at all times. " Some say experience is the best teacher but I believe that experience is the only teacher. I have been awakened to learn of God's love for me only by the experience of my dependence on that love. At first I could not be sure of His direction for me in my life, but now I see that if I am to be bold enough to ask for His guidance, I must act as if He has provided it. I frequently ask God to help me to remember that He has a path for me.

CHAPTER 8.

SUFFERING AS CHRIST'S FOLLOWERS

Christians scholars see the suffering in the light of a type of perfection, where the fires of affliction forge the quality of Christian character in then individual believer. Suffering can be evil but not absolute evil, since it is also a means by which the Holy Spirit increases Christ- likeness. Let me explain that a little more clearly. Christians may experience trails, afflictions, temptation and sufferings. However, to see them as something within the will of God for his or her life, that Christian must have an ever enlarging view of God and his preemptive process.

Men and women whom Christ calls to faithfulness and holiness are drawn into battle with their defects of character and all its influences in contrast to divine progress. Sometimes suffering is a direct result of the believers defective nature or the defects of nature of those closest to them. At time we resist his Spirit, and attempt to shift the blame on to someone or something else, even when it is obvious that the person has caused his or her suffering.

Psalm 32 portrays the response of a person who came up an honest dealing with their own defect o character. " When I kept silent, my bones wasted away through my groaning all day long. For day and night you hand was heavy upon me, my strength was sapped as in the heat of summer. Then I acknowledged my defect to you and did not cover up my iniquity. I said : "I will confess my transgressions to the Lord'- and you forgave the guilt of my wrongdoing,"

Of course not all suffering in the life of a Christian is as a result of their defects of character. It is necessary to consider alongside retributive and disciplinary suffering the complementary principle of educational suffering. God often afflicts his people for his purpose of teaching, chastening and corrections from his hand. And although we may suffer pain, and anguish, God is using it all to teach us how to be his people.

We are called to love and because God loves us, and we love, then in proportion we must suffer and choose to suffer for love. C.S. Lewis wrote in the book 'The Problem of Pain:' "God whispers to us in our pleasures, speaks in our conscience, but shouts in our pains: it is his megaphone to rouse a deaf world."

Lewis went on to write that pain as God's megaphone is a terrible instrument in that it does not guarantee success in terms of sanctification. We know of this action of declaring something holy. Like the sanctification of bread and wine into the body and blood of Christ, as is reminds us and symbolises in every Christian Mass celebration of the last supper when Christ shared those words:'Do this in commemoration of me.' But in our rebellious nature in our pain and suffering, we find rebellion without repentance. Here is then the rub; what the redemptive effect of our pain and suffering will do is, as Lewis remarked: "... plant the flag of truth within the fortress of a rebellious soul." For the redemptive effect of suffering lies mainly in the tendency to reduce the strength of the rebel will. Lewis pointed out that this differs from the ascetic practice which does just the opposite- they strengthen the will and are only useful in that they enable the will to have some control over our earthly passions. Pain does its redemptive work best shattering man's self sufficiency and allowing him/ her to learn sufficiency that can be found only in God.

Lewis saw the pain as part of man's cure. Man's cure is painful because man is not merely an imperfect creature who must be improved; instead man is a rebel who must lay down his arms. To give up self-will is what Lewis calls "a grievous pain." He continues, "To surrender self-will inflamed and swollen with years of usurpation is a kind of death." (i.e.ursurpation a type of reissueor holding on to power over or forcefully retaining self authority which will kill the soul.)

Lewis understood that self- surrender demands pain. The action of surrendering the will to god, in order to be pure, must be done from-a pure will to obey. This indicated the necessity to die to ourselves in loving God, since more often than not, just when we think we have broken the rebellious self, we find that it is still alive and well. " That this process cannot be without pain is sufficiently witnessed by the very history of the word ' mortification.' Lewis identified four-fifths of man's suffering as being caused by wickedness of mans soul that led them to hurt one another. We shall explore this in greater detail in the next chapter on our shadow self.

Much of man's suffering , Lewis argued, could not be traced to man at all. This led Lewis to the problem of reconciling human suffering with the existence of a loving God. The solution was to stop looking at the issue from a man-centred point of view: " God does not exist for the sake of man. Man does not exist for his own sake, We were made to primarily that we may love God but also that God may love us. Lewis explained much of human suffering in the context of God labouring to make man more loveable.

We have to be redeemed from self-will to God's will: " If tribulation is a necessary element to redemption, we must anticipate that it will never cease till God sees the world to be redeemed or to be not further redeemable." Suffering teaches us that what the world offers was never intended to possess our heart. For the Christian, Christ is the only treasure. Or as Lewis asserted "Our Father refreshes us on the journey with some pleasure inns, but will not encourage us to mistake them as home."

One other important aspect of suffering to consider is the concept that when Christians suffer they are sharing in the suffering of God. This may be hard for non believers to grasp, but one only has to observe nature in all its splendour and realise much in the suffering of a seed as it finally to bloom to flower and how radiant its beauty once the suffering has passed. " Consider the lilies of the field, how they grow; they toil not, neither do they spin and yet I say unto you, That even Solomon in all his glory was not arrayed like one of these. "Consider the lilies" encourages us to trust in the providence of God or the infinite intelligence of the maker of all things if you will.

Whether or not the God of ones own understanding experiences suffering is not at issue. God's impassibility is not in question here .Is it to realistic to imagine that a journey into the heart of God will involve significant experiences of pain? Jesus did not neglect to acknowledge the difficulty of life. He promised, "In this world, you will have trouble." He knows our tendency to panic and worry about days ahead but only God holds the answers to whatever you consider God to be.
The one who is willingly undertakes the kenosis of the incarnation, who loved us even in death, and whose suffering body, mind and spirit, if one caress to contemplate this, is manifested throughout the world cannot be apathetic. The Christian comes after a while to realise that the greatest part of the pain which

Christ suffers is not his, but God's. For God is not sharing his pain as truly as he is sharing God's pain. Then he (Jesus) sees the measure he is privileged to share with his suffering on the cross

In is in the story of the passion and death of Christ on the cross that Christians find meaning to their own suffering. The Christian understanding of God has its roots in an historical event: The cross. The way of history is the way of the cross, and the cross is the way into the Trinity God. It is not creation that leads us to God but the cross. As Charles Ohliock in "The Suffering of God: Hope and Comfort for those Who Hurt." adds: " The model for long suffering is God, so our contemplation of him leads us to persevere. The writer of Hebrews tells us to keep our eyes fixed on Jesus who endured the cross. When we consider this example of long suffering, we are encouraged to follow in his steps.

I recall a prayer from my youth here; God, break me the marble of my heart and from its fragments pave a street, where in my bliss I may meet one who hastens with pierced feet.!" So it's seems from my recall of my indoctrination, loss of faith and renewal of same in my latter years is that "Christians range themselves with God in his suffering; that is what distinguishes them from those who can't buy it." It is not some religious act which makes a Christian what he /she is, but participation in the suffering of God in the life of the world. The death and resurrection of Jesus needs to determine the matter in which Christians relate their experience of suffering in strength and hope. Christian Beker, a researcher and scientific professor at Oxford university assets: " For is just bas the death of Christ embraces the various forms of suffering in our lives, so the resurrection of Christ must be the ground of our hope. "

Thereby, these various forms of suffering are not simply meaningless , because they now have the last world in God's world." Henry Wheeler Robinson was a notable nonconformist English Baptist theologian and Old Testament scholar echoed the idea when he finds the Christian solution isn't the problem of suffering' Its when we suffer, discover that God suffers too,Its then it become more bearable to live through it in one's own life and the lives of others." For Robinson, Gods suffering is redemptive, however, i only as it is revealed and understood in the doctrine of the experience of the cross that it then becomes"The bond of creative fellowship." In fact, suffering offers Christians a possibility of communion with Christ at a deeper level, and gives evidence that they are on the way to the fulfilment of our union with The Lord.

There is no doubt that the Bible indicates that those who follow Christ will suffer. For this thesis and argument is that this suffering is purposeful, even necessary, in the process of sanctification. Scripture use three metaphors to describe the way God uses suffering to increase "Christlikeness" in the faithful.

Firstly from Deutrenomy: "Know that in your heart that a man disciplines his son, so the Lord your God disciplines you. The context of this statement is the warning that Moses gives his people that they be careful to follow all the commands so that they can enjoy the fruits of then promises of God. In recounting the hardships of the people in their desert experience, Moses reminds them that God was humbling them and testing them to see if they would consistently trust in God's provision. God's provision was remarkable, including mana from heaven to eat and clothes that did not wear out tough out the forty years in the desert wanderings. But Moses is concerned that then people would forget the Lord, ansd so he warns them to " continue to observe the command of the Lord your God, walking in his ways and revering him."

J.A Thompson biblical was an Australian Old Testament scholar and biblical; archaeologist pointed out the educational nature of the desert experiences and affirms the methodology God used was unique to one occasion. " Often in the Old Testament God is shown as sending suffering to humble and discipline his servants so that they might learn lessons they would otherwise miss. That includes the testing of Abraham, Job, Joseph, Jeremiah to name but a few." Scholars have commented that such discipline was intended to inoculate reformation and righteousness in the offspring.

The metaphor is taken up in the Book of Proverbs, where the saying stresses that father discipline is evident of his love for his children. The third chapter of the proverbs highlights the childlike trust placed by the man of God in wisdom's sound teaching, leading to obedience. Solomon writes; "My son, do not despise the Lord's discipline and do not resent his rebuke, because the Lord disciplines those he loves, as a father the son he delights in. Not despising means not rejecting, a tough assignment when resentment is a natural reaction to hardship. But to follow the path of resentment would mean negating the key theme of childlike trust. It requires the act of birth, will and the emotions to accept the Lord's discipline. But this acceptance is made easier by the remembrance that the discipline is cloaked in the father's love and delight."

These verses in Hebrews addresses urban Jewish backgrounds of Christians facing difficult times. Christians were asking the question as whether or not their faith in Christ was well placed since their experience in life was filled with such trails and persecution. The author in Hebrews 12:5-11 reminds the reader that their status in God's eyes is that of chosen sons. He quotes Proverbs 3:11-12: as a "word of encouragement" and exhorts his readers to pay attention to it. " My son, do not despise the LORD's discipline or be weary of his reproof, for the LORD reproves him whom he loves, as a father the son in whom he delights. We should embrace God's discipline as His loving care fo us. Our natural posture toward discipline is dislike, avoidance, or worse."

When we encounter hardships, we should be indifferent to them, not become overwhelmed by them but rejoice in them, the idea is not to despise the discipline of the Lord for it indicates the possibility that some Christians may be in danger of ignoring or dismissing the fact that God's sovereign hand is at work in their adversities and suffering as well as in their joys and pleasures.

CHAPTER 9.

REFINING GOLD & PRUNING VINES

Sometimes Christians going through adversity and suffering might become overwhelmed. Perhaps it is because they were never disciplined by loving Father in their youth or they were let down through their own defects of character. Whatever the reason, they could become discourage to the point of despondency and even deep depression. (In my case, it was in such a state after many tragic circumstances in my life that I tried to drink my way out of it as God seemed to not be there in my life at the time.)-Not keeping faith with God despite his seeming absence at the time is a great mistake. Christians going through trouble have to keep in mind that the God who tests them is also the god who helps them. His promise is to never test beyond their strength but always to provide grace suffice net enough for the occasion of adversities. As Paul said " God is faithful. He will not let you be tempted beyond what you can bear."

The challenge of hardship and suffering, persecution and adversity, temptation and trails, need not drive Christians to despair. The evil one, in our defects of character, that shadow self, is content to leave most of his subjects in the superficial 'peace' of a spiritual apathy and ignorance. So by standing up and being counted as on in the company of the Lord we are sure to be wounded by the arrows which are constantly directed at Christ himself. These sufferings offer proof that those who endure them belong to the family of God.

The next metaphor relates to God's corrective work in the lives of his people is like that of a metalworker refining gold. The image of te refining, using appropriate terminology, is found in the Old Testament

The believer's faith is "tested by fire" through trials for a specific purpose: "These trials will show that your faith is genuine. It is being tested as fire tests and purifies gold—though your faith is far more precious than mere gold. So when your faith remains strong through many trials, it will bring you much praise and glory and honour on the day when Jesus Christ is revealed to the whole world" (1 Peter 1:7). Peter asserts that trials serve to authenticate our faith by deepening it and strengthening our commitment to Jesus.

Testing by fire is part of the metalworker's process to determine the quality of metal and remove all impurities. A goldsmith or silversmith must repeatedly heat the raw metals to extremely high temperatures until they melt. The contaminants rise to the surface in this liquid state and are skimmed off. Only after this refining process of separating the precious elements from the cross can a pure, valuable, and useful object be formed.

The Bible contains many references to God as the refiner who tests His people's hearts in the fire of adversity. When Peter penned his message, he may have had the suffering of Job in mind. Amid his horrendous ordeal, Job said of God by faith, "He knows where I am going. And when he tests me, I will come out as pure as gold" (Job 23:10).

Through the prophet Isaiah, God spoke to the remnant of Israel, "I have refined you, but not as silver is refined. Rather, I have refined you in the furnace of suffering" (Isaiah 48:10). To an end-times group of Jewish survivors, the Lord declared His purpose again: "I will bring that group through the fire and make them pure. I will refine them like silver and purify them like gold. They will call on my name, and I will answer them. I will say, 'These are my people,' and they will say, 'The Lord is our God'" (Zechariah 13:9).

If you find yourself asking, "Why God? Why are You allowing this suffering?" Remember this: being tested by fire will make you stronger and purer in faith as you remain steadfast through hardship. We can have hope and courage in the face of adversity. if we understand that, through it all, God is working His purposes for our good Romans 8:28). James held that a Christian who perseveres under trial is blessed "because when he has stood the test, he will receive the crown of life that God has promised to those who love him" (James 1:12)). Faith that stays true through every fiery test is more valuable than the finest, purest gold. God sends trails to strengthen our trust in him so that our fith will not fail. Our trails keep us trusting, they burn away our self confidence and drive us to our Saviour.

The affliction or persecution will reduce our faith to ashes. Fire does not destroy gold, it removes combustible impurities… Like a jeweller putting his most precious metal on a crucible, so God proves us in the furnace of trail and affliction. The genuineness of our faith shines from the fire to his praise. God delights to call forth his champions to meet great temptations, or make them bear crosses of more than ordinary weight; just as commanders in war put men of most valour and skill upon the hardest services. God sees some strong, furious trails upon a strong Christian.

Pruning is perhaps the most contrary to common-sense of the three metaphors. For in a certain way it pictures a more drastic and potentially harmful activity. Pruning, simple put, is a cutting off, similar to purging metals of impurities by fire, but pruning it is not always impurities or unhealthy growth that is removed. Sometimes the gardener will intentionally cut off healthy growth in order to shape the plant a certain way. From a gardening standpoint, pruning is a double edged sword, either helping or hindering the plant or tree according to if, where, when, how and why it is applied.

When properly executed, a variety of benefits can occur from pruning. A typical example is a council clean up of vegetation. The benefits include reducing risk of branch and stem breakage, providing a better clearance for vehicles and pedestrians, improving the health and appearance of the plant, enhancing the landscape view, and increasing flowering. However, when performed improperly, pruning can harm the tree's health, stability, and appearance. Still all plant experts warn of the consequences of not conducing a regular pruning program. These include the increasing risk of branch and stem failure, developing low, aggressive limbs, forming dominant stems, creating defects such as diseased bark and dead branches, and developing obstructed landscapes. One of the most beneficial results of pruning is that it encourages plants and trees to grow with strong structure.

In horticultural terms, pruning is a tribute to the potential of a branch. It is an acknowledgement that it is already fruitful and that it has ever greater potential to be more fruitful in the future. Looked at in this way, pruning is not only a mark of favour, it is a mark of expectation on the part of the plant, vine, or tree grower.

The parable of the vine was used by Jesus to describe the importance of both abiding and pruning in the Christian experience. John 15:1-8 records the beginning of Jesus' second upper room discourse and the last major teaching section of the gospel. The image of the vine was one of the supreme symbols of Israel. A great golden vine trailed over the temple porch, and the coinage minted in Israel around the time of the revolt against Rome AD 68-70 incorporated the vine symbol. There are also a number of Old Testament citations to this image, particularly in the psalms and the prophets. Psalm 80 speaks of Israel's exodus experience as "a vine out of Egypt" and her flourishing in Palestine as a dominant vine: "The mountains were covered with the shade, the mighty cedars with its branches. It sent out its boughs to the Sea, its shoots as far as the River."

In Isaiah 27:2 Israel is described as 'a fruitful vineyard," and in Jeremiah 2 :32 God describes the nation as "a choice vine." However, Ezekiel 15:1-8 describes Israel as a useless vine that God will consume with fire. Hosea 10:1-2 created a similar picture: "Israel was a spreading vine; he brought forth fruits for himself. As the fruit increase, he built more altars, as his land prospered, he adorned his sacred stones. Their heart is deceitful, and no they must bare their guilt."

Isaiah 5:1-7 is the Song of the Vineyard. It refers to the association with the Lord's preservation of a remnant of Zion. God has been about the business of protecting and nurturing his vineyard people, but in 5:1-7 the picture is one of an unfruitful vine. Even though grace has been expended on behalf of the people, the result has been only unpalatable grapes. Nothing was left undone to guarantee a sound crop. As was biblically exclaimed by God: " What more could have been done for my vineyard than I have done."

God had great expectations for the vineyard, building a watchtower for its protection and a wine vat to store the crop. But all God found was bad fruit. It is described this way: "Fruitlessness does not merely violate the Lord's formal intention, it contradicts his heart."

There are six woes that the people of the vineyard ultimately suffer for their transgressions in not attending to God vineyard in accord with his plan. There were those more interested in gaining more than their fair share is in the first woe. They go beyond even the desire to be well off; they want as much as they can possibly attain until nothing is left and they are left alone. The other mistake is implicated as oppressing one's neighbours. Understand that land was livelihood, as well as living space. This is an agricultural society. Defrauding someone of his land made him destitute. The only means left to survive is to work for the new owner, which in effect made him a slave.

The second woe addresses debauchery engaging in sensual extravagance. Here are people who burn both ends of the candle to keep up their schedule of drunken bouts. They wake early with a craving for drink and stay up late filling there insatiable thirst. This is not a description of the hardened alcoholic, it is a description of the unrestrained man pursuing sensual pleasure. Pleasure of the flesh is all that drives him.

The third woe is deceit. We don't have here another group of people with a different sin from the others; rather, they accomplish the other sins through deceit. They are pulling along their carts of sin with ropes of deceit. They are working at defrauding and debauchery through lying, hypocrisy, and trickery.

The fourth woe moves us into a worsening condition of reversing the moral order. It is one thing to act badly and admit that it is bad; it is another to act badly and proclaim it as good. But you can see the progression of how this occurs. When a people commit sin over and over, either that behaviour will break down or it will become assimilated into the accepted order. We could spend all night with that one: making up a short list of what society has assimilated as, not only acceptable behaviour, but good. How are we able to turn what was once regarded as evil into being regarded as good. That's easy. We've made man as wise as God.

The fifth woe engages those who regard themselves to be wise and clever in their own sight. This applies to philosophy, and the religious mission of some of the so called faithful . The belief that personal experience, conscience, and reason should be the final authorities. The false belief that religious authority lies not in a book, person, or institution, but in ourselves. We put religious insights to the test of our hearts and minds, upholding the free search for truth: "l will not be bound by a statement of belief." A motto that does not ask anyone to subscribe to a creed. The premise that one has a free faith is like saying that we need no input from God.

Finally, the sixth woe is a mockery of God's people-heroes at drinking wine and champions at mixing drinks, who acquit the guilty for a bribe, but deny justice to the innocent as good.
Comparing to the bad fruit of Isaiah Old Testament woes and betides, is the evidence of the righteous and Christlike character in the lives of those who follow Jesus. This fruit is radically different than the stinking fruit of Isiahs account as Christians today are mean to be like branches on a vine, According to Jesus' words in John 15, the branch must remain firmly attached to the stem of the :vine, or it will wither and die, and ceae to bear fruit. Jesus said:

"Remain in me and I will remain in you. No branch can bear fruit by itself; it must remain in the vine. Neither can you bear fruit unless you remain in me. I am the vine; you are the branches. If a man remains in me and I in him, he will bear much fruit; apart from you can do nothing. If anyone doe not remain in me, he is like a branch that is thrown away and withers, such branches are picked up, thrown into the fire and burned,."

"Pruning is an action designed to inflict the minimum of damage on the vine or plant while achieving the maximum enhancement of its potential." (Statement from Alister McGrath in his book " Suffering and God".) Mc Grath continues; " Those who suffer may well be those who bear the most effective witness and those who bare the most fruit in and through their Christian lives."

Bruce Milne, in the 'Message of John' page 221 : stated "In the clearing off of branches and the cleaning up of others, the gardener is exposing those that are dead and encouraging fruitfulness among those that are living. In pruning God uses hard circumstances and trails. None of these appear pleasant at the time, but th eresult is the production of a harvest."

Milne continues: " It is commonplace both of horticulture and Christian experience that the harder the pruning, the greater the fragrance and beauty which will later be released. Our heavenly Father is hungry fro the fruit from the vine, an in order to produce it will often in the pruning cut deeper than we should ever have chosen. At the harvest, both the sower and the reaper may be glad together."

In order for a branch to grow it must be connected to its life giving sap from the vine or it withers and dies. The vine grower is aware of which of the branches need the pruning of dying wood in order to remain a healthy part of the vine.And he knows how to to prune branches that remain so that they can bear even more fruit. Left to itself a vine will produce excessive and unproductive growth in the branches. Extensive pruning is essential for maximum fruitfulness.

Marcus Dodds, in "The Gospel of John Volume 2, The Exposi-
tions," describes the pruning work that God does as a fruitful
gardener: "The branch is not left to nature. It is not allowed to
run out in every direction, to waste its life in attaining size.
Where it seems to be doing grandly and promising success, the
knife of the vinedresser ruthlessly cuts down the flourish, and
the fine appearance lies withered on the ground. But the vin-
tage justifies the husbandman.

Suffering to the belief of the Christian sometimes does the
pruning work. McGrath describes it as " cutting off spurious
growth which might be of no value or stopping shoots which,
were they to grow further, would weaken the vines." Pruning
hurts, and when you prune a plant you can see the wound that
the pruning inflicts on it. But good pruning is never arbitrary
or pointless, much less vindictive in its intent. Pruning is an
action designed to inflict the minimum of damage too the vines
whilst achieving the maximum enhancement of its potential.
Mc Grath continues:" Those who suffer may well be those
who bear the most excessive witness and those who bear the
most fruit through their Christian lives." In both the development of Christian character and the progress of Christian mission, God acts on their soul to increase their fruitfulness. Of-
tentimes this action takes place through the trials and afflictions that confront the lives of Christians. The pruning that suffering provokes is meant for the good of the Christians themselves as well as the kingdom work to which they are called. In
both, the aim is a healthy growth toward productive life.

In summary, all the metaphors dealt with herein describe negative process with a positive outcome. The discipline of a child
and the ultimate benefit in the guidance and love of a father,
the refining of ones defects of character and the harsh

cutting away of egocentric behaviour in preference to the good character and effective living for the good of all under Godly husbandry.

The discipline, the refining and the pruning- all these evokes a positive result: the child's good, the ore's purity of soul, and the vines fruitfulness. This is the nature of God's use of suffering in the life of believers.

CHAPTER 9.

THE SHADOW SELF IN OUR NATURE

To properly understand the shadow and it's nature, we first "have to explore one's id." So who do we refer to understand this better than the works of Carl Yung on the subject of shadow-self. "Your id is the instinctual part of your personality that exists from the moment you're born; it's the drive you feel for desire, impulse, the need for food, shelter, companionship, and aggression. The id is driven by impulse, desire, instant gratification, and the avoidance of pain and discomfort. Sigmund Freud explained the id as an unconscious force within us, writing:

"It is the dark, inaccessible part of our personality, what little we know of it we have learned from our study of the dreamwork, and, of course, the construction of neurotic symptoms and most of that is of a negative character, and can be described only as a contrast to the ego. We approach the id with analogies: we call it a chaos, a cauldron full of seething excitations. . . It is filled with energy reaching it from the instincts, but it has no organisation, produces no collective will, but only a striving to bring about the satisfaction of the instinctual needs subject to the observance of the pleasure principle."

When we are born, we are born with our id; however, as we mature and begin to orient ourselves in the world, we develop our "ego." Where the id is the search for pleasure and the avoidance of pain, the ego is how we decide our place in the reality of the world around us and how we choose to present ourselves to the world based on each of our experiences, values, and beliefs. In Freudian psychology, the ego is the mind's way of assessing the external world and orienting itself according to what it observes and in alignment with what it judges most appropriate.

This is in contrast to the id, which acts according to pleasure seeking and pain avoidance. The ego mediates the id in delaying gratification and making executive decisions not to act on every impulse but to act in alignment with our values and how we think we *should* behave, rather than how we *want* to behave.

However, as the ego attempts to satisfy the impulse of the id in ways it can justify in the context of reality, there is a risk that it will disguise the desires of the id with unconscious rationalisation. In other words; as the ego attempts to balance pleasure seeking with acting in a way it believe is conducive of being a good person, the ego can warp reality to create stories that validate the impulses of the id and the behaviours that come from those impulses. This is something we have to be on the lookout for. An example of this is the person who eats an entire cake while telling themselves that they deserve it for doing so well on their diet this week.

As humans, we tend to warp reality to serve the impulses of our id, and this behaviour is something we should be aware of. As children, we are consumed by our id, we act on every impulse, we look to avoid all sources of pain, and in that state, the balance of ego and id are almost entirely towards id. As we mature, we learn that not all impulses are constructive and that not all pain is to be avoided. The more we experience and the more we learn, the better we are able to tell the difference.

This is part of wisdom. The ability not only to decide what we should and should not avoid, despite the pressure of the id, but to combine it with the discipline to act on that understanding. With a better understanding of the id and the ego, we can better understand the concept of 'the shadow.' The intimate threat of the darkness of our ego-self will in my view.

Jung explained that the shadow is a cognitive blind spot of our psyche, an undercurrent of who we are that we're completely unaware of; it's an element of our own nature that exists in our unconscious and is made from our repressed desire, ideas, instincts, weaknesses, and shortcomings.It's the gap between the ego and the id. More specifically, the shadow is caused by the resistance that comes from the differences in the life our ego consciously has us live to fit into the world around us and the behaviour our id draws us towards. Jung described the shadow as *"the thing a person has no wish to be."*

An easy way to check the nature of our shadow is to look at others and find out the qualities you like the least. These are often qualities you dislike in yourself and push down or avoid —this is called projection and can lead us to have a warped perception of the people around us.

While we may not like what we see when we begin to look at our shadow, it's exploration is important for personal (soul) progress and purification:

"The meeting with oneself is, at first, the meeting with one's own shadow. The shadow is a tight passage, a narrow door, whose painful constriction no one is spared who goes down to the deep well. But one must learn to know oneself in order to know who one is."

When we feel the pull of our id, and that pull is in conflict with our ego and the person we want to be, this friction is where the shadow presents itself. The risk of the shadow is that it projects itself unconsciously, meaning that it can seep into our thoughts and our actions without us knowing. We may get defensive, we may protest too much about something we actually desire internally, we might lash out at people, or we may use our ego to generate stories that validate the needs of the id and, by extension, the shadow.

In The Archetypes and the Collective Unconscious, Jung wrote: *"A man who is possessed by his shadow is always standing in his own light and falling into his own traps...living below his own level."* However the shadow presents itself, there is a good chance it will be destructive to a greater or lesser extent and have an impact on our lives and our wellbeing. Many of the self-destructive behaviours we inflict on ourselves are caused by the struggle of the shadow. Some addictions are driven by the conflict we experience.

As Stevenson wrote in the story of Jakyll and Hyde, man is not one but truly two; he has a conscious personality and a shadow, each of which often battles for supremacy within his mind.

Man has to realise that he possesses a shadow which is the dark side of his own personality; he is being compelled to recognise his "inferior function", if only for the reason that he is so often overwhelmed by it, with the result that the light world of his conscious mind and his ethical values succumb to an invasion by the dark side. The whole suffering brought upon man by his experience of the inherent evil in his own nature – the whole immeasurable problem of "original sin", in fact – threatens to annihilate the individual in a welter of anxiety and feelings of guilt." – Erich Neumann

Before we look at accepting the shadow and assimilating it into who we are, it's worth taking a moment to reflect on what the shadow can do for us. Within its chaos and impulse, the shadow may also contain a number of qualities and potentials that can help round out our character and personality. For example, if you believe that being assertive or aggressive makes you a bad person, you may have allowed other people to push your boundaries while you said nothing, not wanting to cause trouble. However, your shadow may contain a nature that is assertive, a nature that you can feel push back angrily when you are being pushed by others. If this is the case, then you can learn to harness this element of your shadow so that when you're in a position that requires strong boundaries or negotiation, you have the ability to say no and hold your group.Other examples could include allowing ourselves to express how we're feeling if we've grown up believing that expressing our feelings is a weakness.

Our shadow can help us understand others; when we know our own shadow and see hints of it in other people, we can be more compassionate about what they're feeling. Whatever the nature of your shadow, knowing it will help you accept it, and accepting it will not only loosen its hold over you; it will also begin to unlock its potential.

Carl Jung said: *"There is no generally effective technique for assimilating the shadow. It is more like diplomacy or statesmanship and it is always an individual matter. First one has to accept and take seriously the existence of the shadow. Second, one has to become aware of its qualities and intentions. This happens through conscientious attention to moods, fantasies and impulses. Third, a long process of negotiation is unavoidable."*

So what does this mean? Firstly, we have to accept that part of who we are is this mass of undesirable impulse and desire called the shadow. It is part of all of us, and whether we want it to be there or not, it will influence the way we behave and perceive the world around us. Second, we have to learn its nature. This requires self-reflection. As Jung put it, *"conscientious attention to moods, fantasies, and impulses"*.

This attention can be achieved through meditation, to observe the workings of the mind in the present moment, and through practices like journaling, where we write down our thoughts, moods, fantasies, and desires. Both methods are helpful for learning how our mind works, and both will slowly, over time, allow us to learn the qualities of our shadow. Thirdly, and finally, the negotiation—this is the back and forth that we will inevitably have between accepting the shadow and rejecting it and finding out what is useful to us and what is not. This can again be done through meditation, but you will also need to expose the shadow to the world to see which parts feel constructive and which do not. There are a couple of techniques that can help us with this journey with our shadow:

1.Learning to be consciously aware of how we respond to things and to other people will give us insight into what triggers us, what makes us defensive, and what specific traits in others we tend to dislike. These patterns in our behaviour, over time, help us understand the nature of our shadow. So when we feel the urge to instinctively act in response to something or someone, try to catch yourself in the moment and get a feel for why and what you're feeling.

2. Use the qualities you like about yourself to understand the qualities you dislike. If you like being a calm person, look for examples where your calm has broken and what caused the response. If you like being a kind person, look for areas in your life where you tend to be unkind, cold, or lacking compassion. Look for exceptions to the goodness in you and try to understand why that might be. Its about Managing your inner dialogue—we all speak to ourselves, whether it's conscious or

unconscious. The language we use internally will go some way toward influencing how we react externally. Keep an eye on the language and what is being said; it could lead you to some clarity about the nature of your shadow or the stories we tell ourselves to cover up or validate the needs of the shadow.

Finally, there are a few things that can be useful when we're exploring the shadow in ourselves:

Self-compassion is our ability to be understanding of ourselves when we find something about our character we don't like. It's important to understand that everyone has a shadow beneath the version of themselves they decide to show the world. Some are more destructive than others, but we all have them to some degree. Don't kick yourself too hard.

Self-awareness is our ability to understand how we feel and what we're thinking in the moment. Honesty—and our ability to accept what we see in ourselves and see it for what it is, rather than trying to warp it because it may be uncomfortable.

There you have it, Carl Jung's Shadow Self.

Hopefully you can see the benefit of making the unconscious more conscious and using the parts of ourselves we might not want to think about. This shadow work can go a long way towards helping us feel less resistance to the world around us as we begin to understand the reason for that resistance and even harness it for our own benefit. Understanding our own shadow takes honesty, time, and focus but it's well worth the journey. Other examples could include allowing ourselves to express how we're feeling if we've grown up believing that expressing our feelings is a weakness. Our shadow can help us understand others; when we know our own shadow and see hints of it in other people, we can be more compassionate about what they're feeling.

"The shadow, when it is realised, is the source of renewal; the new and productive impulse cannot come from established values of the ego. When there is an impasse, and sterile time in our lives—despite an adequate ego development—we must look to the dark, hitherto unacceptable side which has been at our conscious disposal....This brings us to the fundamental fact that the shadow is the door to our individuality. In so far as the shadow renders us our first view of the unconscious part of our personality, it represents the first stage toward meeting the Self. There is, in fact, no access to the unconscious and to our own reality but through the shadow. Only when we realise that part of ourselves which we have not hitherto seen or preferred not to see can we proceed to question and find the sources from which it feeds and the basis on which it rests. Hence no progress or growth is possible until the shadow is adequately confronted and confronting means more than merely knowing about it. It is not until we have truly been shocked into seeing ourselves as we really are, instead of as we wish or hopefully assume we are, that we can take the first step toward individual reality." -Connie Zweig

Understanding our own shadow takes honesty, time, and focus but it's well worth the journey.

The shadow self is the aspect of our personality that contains everything we have suppressed or disowned, such as our flaws, traumas, desires, and impulses. The shadow self is not inherently bad or evil. It is simply a part of who we are, and it can also hold positive qualities, such as creativity, passion, and intuition. However, if we ignore or avoid our shadow self, it can cause us problems in our life, such as: Low self-esteem and self-acceptance, difficulty in relationships and communication, Unhealthy coping mechanisms and habits, repetitive patterns of self-sabotage and failure, projection of our issues onto others and lack of authenticity and wholeness.

That's why shadow work is so important. Shadow work is the process of bringing our shadow self to our conscious awareness, understanding it, accepting it, and integrating it into our whole self. By doing shadow work, we can heal our wounds, transform our limitations, and unleash our potential. But how do we do shadow work? Here are some steps and techniques that can help you get started on your shadow work journey.

There are many ways to get to know your shadow self, such as: Reviewing your childhood: Think about the messages you received from your parents, teachers, peers, and society about what was acceptable and unacceptable about you. What parts of yourself did you have to hide, repress, or change to fit in or please others? How did these messages affect your self-image and self-worth?

Noticing your shadow in your everyday life: Pay attention to the situations, people, or emotions that trigger you, annoy you, or make you uncomfortable. What do they reveal about your shadow self? What are you afraid of, ashamed of, or angry about? What are you projecting onto others that you don't want to see in yourself?

Doing the "projection mirror" exercise: This is a powerful technique that involves writing down a list of traits or behaviours that you dislike or judge in others. Then, for each item on the list, ask yourself: How do I exhibit this trait or behaviour in myself? How does it serve me or protect me? How does it limit me or harm me? How can I accept it or change it?

Using shadow work prompts: You can use journaling, meditation, or other forms of self-reflection to explore your shadow self using specific questions or prompts. For example, you can ask yourself: What are the things that I don't want others to know about me? What are the things that I don't want to admit to myself? What are the things that I feel guilty or regretful about? What are the things that I secretly desire or envy?

The second step of shadow work is to heal your shadow self. To do this, you need to be compassionate and forgiving, and willing to embrace the parts of yourself that you have rejected or wounded.

There are many ways to heal your shadow self, such as: Healing your inner child: The inner child is the part of you that holds your childhood memories, emotions, and needs. Many of the issues that you face as an adult stem from your inner child being hurt, neglected, or traumatised. To heal your inner child, you need to reconnect with it, listen to it, comfort it, and nurture it. You can do this by writing a letter to your inner child, having a dialogue with it, or doing activities that make it happy.

Humbling yourself: One of the reasons why we resist our shadow self is because of our ego, which wants to maintain a positive and superior image of ourselves. To heal our shadow self, we need to humble ourselves and admit that we are not perfect, that we make mistakes, and that we have flaws. We also need to recognise that we are not better or worse than anyone else, and that we are all connected and interdependent.

Practicing self-love and self-compassion: To heal our shadow self, we need to love and accept ourselves unconditionally, without judgment or criticism. We need to treat ourselves with kindness, understanding, and forgiveness, especially when we are struggling or suffering. We need to acknowledge our feelings, validate our needs, and celebrate our strengths.

Seeking professional help: Sometimes, our shadow self can be too overwhelming or complex to deal with on our own. In that case, we may need to seek professional help from a therapist, counsellor, or coach who can guide us through our shadow work process. They can provide us with a safe and supportive space, as well as tools and techniques, to help us heal our shadow self.

The third step of shadow work is to integrate your shadow self. To do this, you need to be creative and courageous, and willing to express and embody the parts of yourself that you have discovered and healed. There are many ways to integrate your shadow self, such as: Developing new habits and skills: One of the benefits of shadow work is that it can help you uncover hidden talents, abilities, and passions that you have repressed or neglected. To integrate your shadow self, you can develop new habits and skills that align with your true self and your purpose. For example, if you have discovered that you have a creative shadow, you can start painting, writing, or playing an instrument.Changing your mindset and behaviour: Another benefit of shadow work is that it can help you transform negative patterns, beliefs, and emotions that have been holding you back or causing you problems. To integrate your shadow self, you can change your mindset and behaviour to reflect your new awareness and understanding. For example, if you have discovered that you have an angry shadow, you can learn to manage your anger in healthy ways, such as breathing, meditating, or communicating assertively.

Sharing your shadow with others: A final benefit of shadow work is that it can help you improve your relationships with others by being more authentic, honest, and vulnerable. To integrate your shadow self, you can share your shadow with others who are supportive, respectful, and trustworthy. For example, if you have discovered that you have a fearful shadow, you can open up to your friends, family, or partner about your fears and ask for their support.

Shadow work is not easy, but it is rewarding. By doing shadow work, you can heal your shadow self, integrate it into your whole self, and become a more balanced, fulfilled, and empowered person. If you are interested in shadow work, you can start by following the steps and techniques outlined in this book. You can also find more resources, such as other books, podcasts, or online courses, that can help you with your shadow work journey. Remember, shadow work is a lifelong process, not a one-time event. You will always have a shadow self, and it will always have something to teach you. The more you do shadow work, the more you will grow and evolve as a person. So, don't be afraid of your shadow. Embrace it, heal it, and integrate it. It is a part of you, and it is a part of your greatness.

But what of the whole, the collective, the community in which we live? This world at large, the world of the darkness of the night of the soul, scarred by the horrendous events of the 20th century, of wars, mass murders, atomic bombs and megalomaniac leaders who caused more pain and suffering on humanity than any other time in the history of man.

Is the new light of the 21st century to be an age of enlightenment for man or a continuous repeat of the same? Are we to be any closer to God through all our introspection ? Is it to be a soul search and personal sacrifice like that of past biblical heroes like the understanding of the wisdom of Solomon, King David, and the sufferings and acceptance of Job, or the love of St Peter and St. Paul, in offering themselves in an ultimate duplicate sacrifice, following the sacrificial lamb act of Jesus in his passion and death on the cross. An act of personal sacrifice for the wellbeing of humanity and the forgiveness of sin, or as I prefer to call it mistakes of the defects of character of the individual man.

It it to be just a one man show of self analysis of living life to ones maker as a living example to other by actions in sacrifice for our fellow man or can it become a united front of being all as one in collective action, collective sacrifice, for the fulfilment of God's intent, whatever one and all perceive this to be?

It must be then to draw some conclusions on the nature and embodiment of good intent by the collective as well as the individual if we are to progress towards what is built within each and every individuals DNA; a progression towards fulfilling the good intent of our perception of God's plan, an evolutionary nature to fulfil or a further fall into darkness of self destructive behaviour and ultimate destruction in death of the individual light for future generations living and hope and ultimately the world.

In my contemplation of what has been stated in this chapter and former considerations, I well may have called this book " A New Way of Seeing" In that theme then it is time to draw some conclusions on this thesis of sacrificial introspection, we have to look back a little to move forward a lot.

CHAPTER 11.

TO CRY IN THE SUFFERING CHRIST

So in the previous chapters we have reached the standpoint of introspection of the suffering of the individual for the great good of ones own soul, giving reason for or part in the plan of God. But what of Gods plan for humanity as a whole? So where to go to get some clarity on this, to throw a light into the darkness to see what can be gained for our part in the world at large.

In Jurgen Moltham's 'The Crucified Christ' (1974) he points to the doctrine of the trinity and defines the relevance of human suffering.Throughout the book he argues that the Christian church's identity and relevance are intimately tied with that Christian theology on suffering of crucified Christ through the significance of Christ's suffering for the created order. Moltmann argues that the crucifixion of Jesus was first and foremost a Father, Son and Holy Spirit event in which all three persons of the Godhead participate in Christ's identification with, and redemption of, the suffering of the world. In arguing the cross as an event within the life of one God who exists as three persons in one, the author reengages the ancient teachings of the existence of evil in a God created world and that God can suffer, a Christian tradition that had previously deemed inadequate and misleading.

The result is a Trinitarian theology of the cross which, in exposition of the nature of the relationship between the divine suffering and the suffering of the world, is judged to be an innovative and substantive contribution to theological discussion on the problem of the existence of evil in a God created world involving God's relationship to the suffering of humanity and creation.

From a world view on the suffering of humanity a good case point is the 20th century where evil ruled the world for most decades and humanity suffered immensely. The nineteenth century gave way to the twentieth with an air of expectation that humanity had reached a golden age of maturity. Despite of this optimism the more scholarly could see clouds on the horizons with the new age "A certain buoyancy of spirit was evident in most schools of thought at the beginning of the century, a buoyancy which has been more and more weighed down as the world had become increasingly disjointed and unstable." (Macquarie'University study 1988-99).

Even the most casual glance at recent history reveals that the optimism was unfounded. And the first major flaw in humanities optimism came in April 1912 when the Titanic, on its maiden voyage to New York from Southampton struck an iceberg and by the following morning the 'unsinkable' ship had sunk. Not only had the flagship of the White Star line been lost but also the hope as an aspirations of those who had confidence in the facts of human engineering, and fully two thirds of the Titanic's passengers and crew also lost their lives that night. The world was stunned at the apparent powerlessness of human ingenuity to prevent a tragedy.

Such optimism was also called into question when, in the aftermath of the world altering event of WW1, of the Spanish flu epidemic ensured. WW1 forced humanity to admit that it had not progressed to the point where human beings were capable of continuous and peaceful coexistence with people of other political, religious or ethic origins. The twentieth century, in fact, witnessed a steady procession of one war after another, one atrocity after another, and one genocide after another. Idi Amin's Uganda, Pol Pot's killing fields of Cambodia, the ethnic cleansing of the Balkans and Rwanda have all followed the horrors of the Western Front and the Jewish holocaust. The incidents   and mat other acts of human inhumanity to man gives rise to the question: How is it possible to engage in theology in the aftermath of Auschwitz, Hiroshima and the Thalidomide children?

Yet, many simply prompt the question of the possibility of engaging in theology. These and other acts of unrestrained inhumanity have provided, yet again, the grounds for the most cited reason given by people for remaining uninterested in Christianity and being unmoved by its teachings. C.S. Lewis in 'The Problem of Pain' (1940:14), has restated the vindication of divine goodness and providence in the view of existence of evil, as a conundrum in the manner that " If God were good, He would wish to make His creatures perfectly happy, and if God, were almighty, he would be able to do what he wished. But the creatures are not happy. Therefore, God lacks either goodness or power or both." It seems that humans are still haunted by the shadows that has been cast but so many uninhibited atrocities over the past century. One might ask: "Where was God when all these evil events were happening and where is he now?" The answer finds amplification in Jerry Irish's (1975) commentary, " where is God now? He is there on the cross- and at Auschwitz, and Memphis, and My Lai, and at all the unmanned places where death reigns through oppression, ignorance and apathy."

And as the twentieth century gave way to the twenty-first, the world was left with no doubt that the question of innocent suffering was not simply a phenomenon confined to obscure and distant 'unnamed places.' The whole world community found itself unavoidably confronted by the reality of events on eleventh of September 2001. Innocent suffering was brought to the very centre of international politics when a group of terrorist hijacked four commercial airlines and deliberately flew them into public buildings in New Work and Washington.

These events caused many of the western world to be struck by a dome of paralysis for several days, such was the scale of devastation. Yet as great as the scale of loss of human lives on that date it is dwarf by other acts of human brutality as has been previously mentioned, like the remains of seven thousand Rwandan Tutsi, and the eleven millions known Jewish victims of the Holocaust . We could go on mention in the mass murder of people by lone gunman in schools, places of worship, centres of entertainment and even shopping centres throughout the western world. The fact remains that even in the present day the innocent suffer even unto death.

The Christian response to the question raised by the suffering of the innocent must be centrally upon Christ-logic in as much as God was reconciling all things in Christ (2 Cor 5:19). Christianity moreover proclaims a 'risen' Christ who's no less present in the world today than at the crucifixion, and no less involved in the redemption of all things now than he always was (2 Cor 5-18). His   immediate involvement to world's problems is no more clearly expressed than in Godfrey Rust's exposition of the events at the World Trade Center September 11, 2001:

"Where is God? Rusk ask.
 His answer.

He was begging
in old clothes in the subway
beneath the World Trade Center
He was homeless in Gaza
imprisoned in Afganistan,
starving in Somalia
dying of aids in a Angolan slum,
Suffering everywhere in this God fast-shrinking world;
And boarding a plane unwittingly in Boston,
heading for a meeting on the 110th floor.
When the time came

He stretched his arms out once again to take
the dreadful impact that would pierce his side,
His last message on his fading cellphone
Once more to ask forgiveness to them all, before
The body fell under the weight of so much evil.

How then is Christian theology to proceed? Throughout the course of the last century increasing numbers of theologians have been drawn to the conclusion that Christian theology must reconsider the question of the suffering God. In may be said that only the suffering God can help his suffering people. A God who reigns in a state of impartial blessedness in heaven cannot be accepted today. " Who is Christ really, for us today?"

If God, as Christians maintain, is reconciling the world through Christ, then Jesus, the one ascent from God, is then the one to whom the Christian church must look for answers to the deeply perplexing questions of human suffering. Accordingly, a truly Christian answer can be nothing other than that which derived from the full account of Jesus' experience of persecution, rejection and crucifixion. His life and ministry, and in particular his cry of being abandoned from the Calvary cross (Mark 15:34), offer a far more convincing response to the problem of suffering than any abstract theological speculation since Christianity proclaims that God himself has entered into the suffering of creation in the person of Jesus of Nazareth. God becomes man in Jesus of Nazareth, he not only enters into the limits of boundaries of this man, but in his death on the cross also enters into the situation of man's God-forsaken.

He humbles himself and take upon himself the eternal death of the godless and the godforsaken, so that all the godless and godforsaken can experience communion with him.

In The Crucified God, Jorgen Moltmann, arguably the best German speaking academic theologian at the end of the twentieth century state: The more theology and the church attempt to become relevant to the problems of the present day, the more deeply they are drawn in the crisis of their own Christian identity. The more they attempt to assert their identity in traditional dogmas, rights and moral notions, the more irrelevant and unbelievable they become. It was Moltmanns observation that the reconciling of the Church's (which may perhaps be called the body of Christ's peoples), identity was essentially the reclining of that Church identity and relevance u in the context of a troubled world grounded in ' an abstract theology of cross and of suffering as in a theology of the crucified Christ, for only the the scandal and mystery of the crucified God can resolve the problem of human suffering."

In Moltmann's theology in the Crucified God, in h short is 'we need to examine the inner development in the life of this man to be able to understand the elementary decisions and impressions which govern his work. So the key question is what are the key experiences which have given this life its unique direction?'

Moltmann's dilemma through all his war experiences and personal suffering came, amid his anguish when he sought comfort and solace in Biblical Psalms. Eventually, he was drawn to the Passion narrative of Christ's crucifixion, and came to a most profound understanding of, and identification with Jesus' cry of being abandoned at the precise moment of his final breaths on the cross: "My God, My God, why have you forsaken me?" (Mark 15:34). Indeed it could be said that Moltmann's faith and theology had grown out of the awareness of that moving significant Bible verse. Whilst he denied that he 'decided for Christ' in the conventional contemporary sense, he concedes that there was a time when he clearly understood Christ had decided for him and that moment is as recorded in Mark 15: 34.

The theology of Moltmann was born out of the wartime experience of suffering and death that surrounded him, and the crucible of life's questions in search for truth and meaning: . ["It come into being in the night of immediate and cruel proximity to death and therefore in the end it is never about learning intellectual games butt about questions of life and death. It does not arise out of peaceful and cheerful awareness of an unshakable certainty in God but out of the abysmal experience of the remoteness of God."

Moltmann's experience and his theology developed out of and inseparable bond of togetherness with the corporate experiences of the German people: As he says in his won words." My biography was shaped , interrupted and radically changed , in a very painful way, by the collective biography of the German people in the last years of the Second World War and by a lengthy imprisonment after it. The individual approach of my faith and ththe ought and therefore also of my theology is embedded n the collective experiences of guilt and suffering in my generation." His experiences of life have caused him to conduct his theological enquiry of that context and those experiences. It was the Godforsaken in the concentrations camps, in the awareness of Auschwitz, that then Lords prayer became relevant to him. For in his teleology he drew on that fact that God himself was in Austchwitz, suffering with the martyred and murdered. To hime any other answer would be blasphemous.

He had reviewed Christ Pentecostal and divine gifts for believers to fulfil their vocation and concluded; that we are not given divine spirituality to flee from the world in a world of religious dreams, but are given the real intent to witness the liberation of Christ in our world of conflicts. The charismatic movement must not become a non political religion let alone a depoliticised one. We must insist that his theological work was written at the time for the times and thus is to be understood as contextual theology set within the context of contemporary life.It is in his philosophy that all understanding of the Crucified God is in Jesus cry uttered in a loud voice (Mark 27:46) It is well noted by this author that nothing other than the articulation of Jesus's confusion, frustration and outrage at his apparent abandonment by God it at issue here.

The argument here is then point of the argument of the relevance of the cross to a suffering world. Here the omnipotent God is revealed in the impotency of the crucified one, and the loves and provision of the Father is known but his resurrection of the one whom was abandoned. This Son's experience of godlessness and godforsaken abandonment is nothing other than his identification with all of those who are also victims of violence-the' godless' ones. The adoption of a discussion of ideas and opinions concerned with or acting through opposing forces is important, for so far as God is revealed in his opposite can he thereby be known in and by the godless and those who are abandoned by God, a knowledge which brings them into a correspondence with God. ["...It is dialectical knowledge of God in his opposite which first brings heaven down to earth for those who are abandoned by God, and opens heaven to the godless." Moltmann.]

Whilst Moltmann's views are one sided, his theology none-theless engages the struggle for truth which liberates in opposition to rejecting all religious and moral principles in the belief that life is meaningless which is oppressive to the truth seeker. So biological theology cannot be timeless or without location. It must forgo correctness in order to be concrete It cannot afford balance, but must take sides and speak one-sidedly. Its intention is not to satisfy itself, but to make a contribution to the healing of everything in church, culture and creation.

Multmann himself writes [It is only in free dialogue that truth can be accepted for the right and proper reason-namely, that it illuminates and convinces as truth. Truth brings about assent, it brings about change without exerting compulsion. In dialogue the truth it frees man and women for their own conceptions and their own ideas. In liberating dialogue teachers withdraw into the circle of brothers and sisters. The pupil becomes the friend. Christian theology would wither and die if it did not continually stand in dialogue like this, and if it were not bound up with a fellowship that seeks this dialogue, needs it and continually pursues it,]

So in Moltmanns viewpoint it is the dialectical knowledge of God in his opposite which first brings heaven down to earth of those who are abandoned by God (or seeming feel they have been abandoned.), that opens up heaven to the godless. It was this author's viewpoint that argued for the existence of an irre-placeable dialectic between the cross and resurrection.

Indeed, the death of Christ on Calvary cross is a unique event in the history of God's self-disclosure to his people, an event of the renunciation of the divine nature, at least in part by Christ incarnation, in which the trinity of Father, Son and Holy spirit in God is thrown open for all to see. Yet, the interpreta-tive key to this event lies within the identity in contradiction that exists in the person of the crucified and the risen Jesus. That is in the fact that it is none other than the godforsaken and abandoned one who is also the god blessed and resurrected one. As a result, the Christian cannot know the relationship to death, judgment and the final destination of the soul of humankind, in the promise of resurrection and eternal life other than through the godforsaken of the Son's abandonment by the Father and his trust in the resurrection to follow, i.e for himself as the incarnate one of the father and ultimately the suffering death and resurrection of his people.

It seems to me that whilst Moltmann defines the suffering of the Son and intimates that God the Father, the creator of all suffers with his Son, as he does with those of us of his creation to this day, the ultimate point of the message overlooked by this theology is the nature of the third person of the Trinity, the Holy Spirit in this.

Notwithstanding the allegations of a tendency towards a one sided and overtly speculative theological methodology Jurgen Moltmann has produced a powerful thesis on the struggle between good and evil in the world, the struggle of God who seemingly abandoned Christ before his death on the cross, and left us also to our own devices of learning experience to trust in his slow work for an overall outcome of spiritual betterment, rather than our defective nature that leads only to sin and death. Whilst Moltmann sought to articulate that the centre of Christian theology should be nothing other than Christ's experience of god-forsakenness and abandonment during the veneers of his crucifixion, his claim is that such understanding led him to that monstrous phrase "the Crucified God."

In his theological belief the centre of Christian theology should be Christ suffering as an ultimate in overcoming our natural instinct. In the eyes of Christianity it is through forgiveness of our sinfulness, through Christ ultimate sacrifice to save us that allows us to be forever with the Father, the Son and the Holy Spirit in his heaven kingdom. This is the point of his ultimate plan for us all along.

It should not be overlooked that the Christian theology is a three pronged Godhead where Moltmann agonising account of Christ being forsaken and abandoned by God fits more into his own sufferings in WW11 and what he witnesses in the suffering and seeming abandonment of the Jewish peoples under the horrors of Nazi Germany, and not on the totality of the Trinity. He focus in his 'Crucified God' more on the Son and Father, the two persons of the Trinity, rather than including the third person's influence, that of the saving power of divine revelation of the Spirit.

So it is that whilst Christ (as revealed biblically and in historical accounts and non biblical theological text,) suffered, died and was buried for the sins of mankind, and it is also through this Christ that we ourselves are redeemed to salvation. If we only have faith to believe and are willing to embrace that belief in the 'risen' Son of God, the second person of the Trinity, and also take on the Holy Spirit, the third person of the Trinity, the divine Spirit that God grants us through the crucifixion to save us from ourselves will be revealed.

In Christianity, when the sacrifice of Christ is reenacted as the Mass of the Last Supper, the priest offers the bread and wine as the body and blood of Christ, to take and eat just as Jesus did with his apostles when he uttered:" take ye and eat, for this is my body and this is my blood, do this in commemoration of me." The priest then adds: "The mystery of faith."

It is difficult to get our head around this but it seem that the infinite Intelligence, the Father of all created a plan, Jesus by his sacrifice on the cross implemented the plan by accepting his suffering and death for humankind, and as a consequence the the spirit of a third person of the Trinity of the Godhead administers the plan.

For it seems that that this Spirit hovers over each and every one of us continually and we need only to embrace it in meditation, prayer and in faith to be guided to God's will.. Then we can reason that suffering is part and parcel of our nature and need of acceptance in gifts of spiritual grace and understanding that will be granted us if we but yield to his will.

So it seems that we are to embrace divine suffering of the One who was abandoned and likewise abandon our will and our defects to God's guidance in accepting Gods plan for us even though we humans suffer. This belief is still shrouded in mystery as is the Trinity of God a mystery of God himself to a great degree.

CHAPTER 12.

EPILOGUE

This book first started on the premise of my own introspection as a cathartic journaling in understanding my former sufferings in life, the suffering of friends and humanity at large, and indeed to get a grip on why we suffer at all. Its a pathway in how we deal with the slings and arrows of outrageous fortune that from time to time befall us. In essence this thesis that has evolved tended to be devised in my mind eye. A formal way for cleansing self of defects that have unwittingly influenced my own life. Instincts we and those which my defective nature in observation has brought influence too .the lives of others. Indeed in research on the subject have found it to be a learning curve in the accepting the consequence of my actions and those of others be they for better or for worse.

It is through these writings that I have come to believe in the power of one greater than self, in the means to a pathway for my betterment, and ultimately for my own salvation. It is to be hoped that through these writings that you might gain some benefit for your own journey inwards and also benefit those whom you can influence in what they come to believe as being vital for their betterment, that of society and humanity at large.

It must be said that from my research the divine all powerful God compensates for human impotence, divine knowing counters human knowledge, whilst divine unlimited goodness guarantees that the lack of love evident within humanity will not triumph. In God's creation we accept that God is love, and that the divine being in Jesus Christ was subject to passion and death out of love for humanity. That God suffered to on the cross as did Christ. That God cried and suffered as we ourselves cry and suffer in our own passions. It is not inconceivable   to me that the Creator might exert passions upon himself by way of inflicted suffering to effect change within the divine being and ultimately within us, even if we don't understand it at the time.

In my former logical linear rote learning Christian up bringing I was drawn to the suffering and death of Jesus, as equally as I was to the Old Testament of the ten commandments of God. It was in a era of black and white thinking, There was no shade of grey in spiritual indoctrination. The whole world was still reeling and renewing after the economics depression and the aftermath of WW11. Personal sacrifice for the good of many was the rule of thumb and people went out of their way to be kind to their neighbour, attend church service on Sundays, give generously to the church, the community and the poor. It seemed to be the norm to us children of the 1950s.

But then came the 1960s and the 1970s in our wild and wooly youth of sex, booze and rock-n-role the development of a youth self begin to reject the old ways of our former upbring-ing in favour of a new materialistic world. Good times out-weighed the old value system of my parents era. It was for me despite suffering from abandonment as a child and witnessing death of love-ones more often than I care to remember, a way of burning painful experiences in favour of have a good time. In essence the child self was more for pleasure seeking than the discipline of the spirit. Whilst from time to time my con-scious got the better of me, the drinking to excess and the pleasure of the flesh seemed more natural to me than what the Christian principles of good living had to offer. To be fair the world at large was on a similar trajectory.

The good time soon passed as I settled down in my late twenties to marriage, the education of children, and the duty of keeping a good wife happy with the material rewards of my hard work. The protestant work ethic was ingrained well by my fathers influence and I realised soon enough that nothing keeps a women happier than to see her husband on the straight and narrow path of being overburden by a heavy home mortgage.

So it was that for the next thirty years I worked my way into material wealth,-with bigger homes, larger business interests, cars, a leisure boat and resort holidays to unwind. Already my daily evening drinking was getting out hand but I believe back then that I had it under control. All seemed rosy in my world until it all turned pear shaped. One tragic event after another unfolded and I lost it all; wife, family, home and business, and the most unkindest cut of all, the suicide of my second eldest son. I tried to drink it all away, and ultimately that landed me in a rehabilitation hospital to try to get my better self back on and even keel again and overcome my depression, anxiety and sense of being totally lost.

[In the death of Christ on the cross we cannot say that the Father also suffered and died. The suffering and dying of the Son, forsaken by the Father, is a different kind of s suffering from the suffering of the Father in the death of his Son... The Son suffers dying, the Father suffers in the death of the Son. The grief of the Father here is just as important as the death of the Son. The fatherlessness of Son is matched by the Soullessness of the father].

I cried out to God many time, tried going to church for direction, turned to pray and meditation, but nothing seemed to work. It seemed like the God that I then understand to be the Supreme being had abandoned me too. The only apparent good thing that had come out of it all, was that I had given up alcohol in fear that I might suicide whilst under the influence.

[Anyone who suffers without cause first thinks that he has been forsaken by God. God seems to him to be the mysterious, in a comprehensible God who destroys the good fortune that he gave.]

It took time to make a change for the better, it came with being led to Alcoholics Anonymous upon leaving Rehab. In truth I had no where else to go and was advised by a patient in the next bed to me in the hospital to go to AA and listen to alcoholics share their experience, strength and hope and to let the message flow over me. He had been a leading Sydney psychiatrist before his retirement and was again suffering a depressive episode. He pointed out to me that in his opinion I was a "dyed in the wool alcoholic" and he confirmed that by saying that "he knew it because when I came to the rehab unit I reminded him of his mental and emotional alcoholic state when he was my age." So it was then that I entered the doorway of AA. I came to believe in a renewed 'spiritual' higher power which I choose as an Infinite Intelligence. I could not see for the God of my Catholic upbringing as the answer for me any more. [In recent times though that view has changed.]. It was whilst I was at my first meeting that I heard the messages that awakened me to my years of alcoholic behaviour. It was a miracle awakening of sorts and soon enough the desire for alcohol left me for good.

In writing these lines I am reminded of the co-founder of AA and his spiritual awakening to become sober a day at a time. Bills Wilson stated: "moments of perception can build into a lifetime of spiritual serenity, as I have excellent reason to know. Roots of reality, supporting the neurotic underbrush will hold fast despite the high winds of the forces which would destroy us, or which we would use to destroy ourselves."

"There was a time in the old Winchester Cathedral that I recall I had always believe in a power greater than myself. I had often pondered these things, I was not an atheist …. For that means blind faith in the strange proposition that the universe originated in a cipher and aimlessly rushes nowhere. My intellectual heroes, the chemists, the astronomers, even the evolutionists, suggested vast laws and forces at work. Despite contrary indications I had little doubt that a mighty purpose and rhythm underlay all. How could there be so much precise and immutable law and no intelligence? Put simply I had ta belief in a Spirit of the universe, who knew neither time nor limitation. But that was as far as I had gone. "

With ministers and world religions, I had parted company right there. To Christ I conceded the certainty of a great man, not too closely followed by those who claimed Him. His moral teaching- most excellent. For myself, I had adopted those parts which seemed conveniently and not too difficult and the rest I disregarded. The wars which had been fought, the burning and deceptions that religious dispute had facilitated made me sick. I honestly doubted whether on balance, the religions of mankind had done any good. Judging from what I had seen in Europe and since, the power of God in human affairs was negligible, the Brotherhood of Man a grim joke. If there as a Devil, he seemed to be of Boss Universal and he certainly had me."

"My friend stood before me, he had stopped drinking and made the point blank declaration that God had done for him what he could not do for himself. His human will had failed. Doctors had pronounce him incurable. Society was about to lock him up. Like myself he had admitted complete defeat.

Then he had, in effect, been raised from the dead, suddenly taken from the scrap heap to a level of life better than he had ever known! Had that power originate in Him? Obviously it had not. There had been no power in him than there was in me at that minute; and this was none at all. That floored me. It began to look as though religious people were right after all. Here is something at work in the human heart which had done the impossible. My ideas about miracles were drastically revised right then. Never mind the rusty past; here sat a miracle directly across the kitchen table, he shouted great tidings. I saw that my friend was much more inwardly reorganised. He was on a different footing. His roots grasped a new soil."

Bill had grandiose notions of what to define as God but his friend suggested something then that seemed a novel idea: He said " Why don't you choose your own conception of God?" His statement melted the icy intellectual mountain in whose shadow Bill had dived and shivered many years. "I stood in the sunlight at last." he said. "It was only a matter of being willing to believe in a Power greater than myself. Nothing more was required of me to make my beginning."

Bill W humbly offered himself to God, and he then understood Him to do as God willed. Bill placed himself unreservedly under His care and direction, admitting for the first time that of himself he was nothing; that without God he was lost. He faced his defective character and became willing to have his new found friendship with God to take them away roots barbs and all. For the rest of his life he remained sober. But that's not the end of his story.

He was to test his thinking with the new God - consciousness within. Common sense would thus become uncommon sense. He was to sit quietly when in doubt, asking God only for direction to meet any problems he would have him do. Never was Bill to pray for himself, except as requested on his usefulness to others, and what might he expect to receive. But it would be in good measure. His friend pointed out to him that when these things were done, he would enter a new relationship with his Creator: That he would have the elements of a way of living which would have the answer to all his problems. Belief in the power of God, plus enough willingness, honesty and humility to establish and maintain the new order of things, were the essential requirements. A price had to be paid which was to be the destruction of his being self centred.

He had been recovering in hospital from the after effects of a depressive episode brought on by his former drinking. He had been thinking about the revolutionary and drastic proposals his friend had mentioned, but the moment Bill accepted them, the effect was electric. There was a sense of victory, followed by such calm and serenity he had never known. There was an utter confidence when he felt he had been lifted up, as though the great clear wind of a mountain top blew through and through. God comes to most men gradually but His impact on Bill was sudden and profound. There was a sense of victory followed by peace and serenity. Bill's friend who had visited him in his kitchen earlier had emphasised the absolute necessity of demonstrating the principles in all his affairs. Particularly it was imperative he was to work with others, as his friend had worked with him. "Faith without works is dead." was the catch cry of St James in his preaching after the death of Jesus. And how appallingly true of the alcoholic. For if an alcoholic failed to perfect and enlarge his spiritual life through work and self sacrifice for others, he would not survive the certain trails and low spots ahead. If he did not work he would surely drink again, an if he drank he would die. With us alcoholics it is just like that.

So Bill Wilson in the company of his fellow co-founder of Alcholics Anonymous back in 1935 started a movement that has held alcoholic worldwide since the foundation of the AA Big Book and steps to sobriety were first introduced to the still suffering alcoholics. The movement goes on to this very day. Bill choose a way of life that mirrored St Paul to a great degree in leading others to God through his many works on a one on one basis with fellow alcoholics and the many books he wrote on the subject of alcoholism and spirituality. At last count in 2020 over 60 million copies of books written by Bill have been sold world wide.

Alcoholics Anonymous: The Story of How Many Thousands of Men and Women Have Recovered from Alcoholism is a 1939 basic text, describing how to recover from alcoholism. It was primarily written by one of the founders of Alcoholics Anonymous (AA), Bill Wilson with two chapters, "To Employers" written by Henry Parkhurst who was an agnostic atheists and the fourth member of the founding fathers of the AA movement.   In the wonderment of helping the suffering souls of the world collectively the AA story of those early pioneers are living proof that humanity as a whole can be changed for the better in the relief of their suffering.

St.Paul is another prime example of self sacrifice for humanity. Paul's letters to the Romans is a powerful exposition of the doctrine of the supremacy of Christ and of faith in Christ as the source of salvation. In his letters to the Corinthians among other things he encourage the Christians of Corinth to reject false teachings, to remain united, to shun immorality, and to strengthen their faith int he resurrection. The evangelist Paul endangered his own life many times in the pursuit of doing the work of God for the suffering souls of humanity. This was paramount in his writings.

Paul writes Colossians to emphasise that Jesus is the fullness of God an that anyone who is in Jesus had received that fullness in him ((Paul 2:9-10).. Paul's goal is to help the original readers and us realise that Christ is enough.He wrote the letter to the Philippians from Rome, where he was in prison. It was written about ten years after the church had ben founded, and three years after Paul had visited there. The personal, affectionate tone of the letter reveals his close relationship with the church and its members. And then their is the main message of the Book of Philippians for the community too be steadfast in faith and the expression of joy.. Philippians is recognised as Paul's joyous epistle and is also known as the "friendship letter" because of its tone.

It seems that it is up to each and every individual who believes in God self to relieve the suffering of other through the promise of faith in God as one in union with him individually and to promote the collective belief to ave tne world of the suffering.

It was Bill Wilsons experience in turning his faith in God to useful purpose centred on the still recovering alcoholic. He wrote many books to encourage others to enter the rooms of AA to a healthy and rewarding life of sobriety and spirituality. Equally St Paul experienced his blindness on the road to Damascus and turned his persecution of the Christians into a belief and zeal of his personal suffering to faithful works for God instead of his former self attempts to destroy the faithful who followed the Way of the cross of Jesus.

This thesis has drawn me back to my experience of sobriety and the many pilgrimage I have been in contact with since that day I first entered a meeting of AA and had a spiritual awakening too. I recall my early experiences on the Camino de Santiago were I was awakened to a lotus flower of creative ideas that has to date, over the past decade, resulted in the production of twenty books, three album of songs and that I had no idea in my former life that I would be inspired to do.

My books and songs traverse many genre of biographical works, autobiographical introspections, humour, novelist ideal and political consciousness. I, with the guiding hand of my muse create these in sure and certain reward of coming to terms with my own demons and the hope that my inspiration be of benefit to other souls who may gain from my efforts.

And so this thesis comes to and end and in my review I feel sure that I may be one step closer today to doing the work that God may grant me in the future, as equally He may grant you too.

About the Author.

Doug McPhillips, poet, singer, songwriter, and author, commenced his journey of discovery over a decade ago after life-changing experiences.

The many tracks he has traversed through the Northern Hemisphere and down under in Australia and New Zealand have resulted in the facts and fiction of this novel.

Doug has recorded and sang songs interrelated to his many works with majestic melodies in a true Australian style

Doug has written several novels, two books of poems, a travel guide and three albums of his songs all inspired by his adventurers.

Doug is an adventurer who divides his time between family and friends, his creative pursuits, and those who benefit most from his efforts and experience.

Reference material:

Holy Bible New International Version Hodder & Stoughton 1983.

A telescopic View of suffering: a Christian Perspective. Judith Gracia & Jessica Selwyn, NCC Review- February 2022.

How should we suffer? Meditation on Christian Responses to the problem of suffering. Colby H. Dickinson, Chicago, Academia, 2020.

Therapeutic Theodicy? Suffering, Struggle and the Shift from God's Eye View, Amber L Griffon,, University of Konstanz, Germany March 2018.

Santiago Traveller: My pilgrimage to a Hidden Treasure. IngramSpark publishers published Doug McPhillips 2018.

The Sword of Discernment: A journey of the spirit. I ngramSpark publishers Doug Mcphillips 2014.

Paul and the Self: Apostolic Teaching for Personal.Suffering. Knox Chamblin, Eugene Or: Wipf and Stock Publishers 2002.

Suffering and God,Alister E. Mc Grath, Zondervan Publishers, 1992.

Mrcus Dodds, Gospel of John, Vol 2, The Expositors Bible, Hodder and Stoughton 1891.

Twelve steps and Traditions of Alcholics Anonomous, the AA Grapevine, April 1953.

The Crucified God, Jurgen Moltmann, Harper & Row, 1974.

* 9 7 8 0 6 4 8 6 2 1 4 5 4 *